Authentic Spiritual Mentoring

Nurturing Younger Believers Toward Spiritual Maturity

LARRY KREIDER

Regal

From Gospel Light
Ventura, California, U.S.A.

D0112057

Published by Regal
From Gospel Light
Ventura, California, U.S.A.
www.regalbooks.com
Printed in the U.S.A.

Library of Congress Cataloging-in-Publication Data
Kreider, Larry.
  Authentic spiritual mentoring / Larry Kreider.
    p. cm.
  ISBN 978-0-8307-4413-8 (trade paper)
  1. Spiritual direction. I. Title.
  BV4408.5.K74 2007
  253.5'3—dc22

                                                    2007034011

        1 2 3 4 5 6 7 8 9 10 / 10 09 08 07

Rights for publishing this book in other languages are contracted by Gospel Light Worldwide, the international nonprofit ministry of Gospel Light. Gospel Light Worldwide also provides publishing and technical assistance to international publishers dedicated to producing Sunday School and Vacation Bible School curricula and books in the languages of the world. For additional information, visit www.gospellight worldwide.org; write to Gospel Light Worldwide, P.O. Box 3875, Ventura, CA 93006; or send an e-mail to info@gospellightworldwide.org.

Praise for

Authentic Spiritual Mentoring

Larry Kreider has presented to us an excellent biblical presentation of the principles, value and purpose for authentic spiritual mentoring. Every Christian and church leader who wants to reach his or her maximum potential needs to read this book.

Dr. Bill Hamon
Bishop, Christian International Ministries Network, Santa Rosa Beach, Florida

Mentoring, fathering and raising up healthy spiritual posterity is the most urgent task of the Church today. *Authentic Spiritual Mentoring* gives scriptural keys that can help any serious Kingdom-advancing church or ministry move to a higher level of effectiveness.

George Bakalov
Founder and Overseer, Harvest Breakthrough Network International, Inc. Apple Valley, Minnesota

Larry Kreider is a father in the Church today, and he writes out of who he is and out of the practical experience he has gained over the years. This book is a must for those who are mentoring or discipling others.

Barbara J. Yoder
Senior Pastor, Shekinah Christian Church, Ann Arbor, Michigan

Authentic Spiritual Mentoring is timely and will find a large readership in the Body of Christ, especially among marketplace ministers. It powerfully presents the relational base for cultural transformation and for extending the kingdom of God in the earth.

Jim Hodges
Apostolic Leader, Federation of Ministers and Churches International, Denton, Texas

Authentic Spiritual Mentoring covers practical topics that are not found in other books on this key topic. After teaching mentoring for years in seminary and churches, I have used every helpful book that was available. This book would have been at the top of my list.

Dr. Joseph Umidi
Founder, Lifeforming Leadership Coaching, Virginia Beach, Virginia

We have many teachers but few fathers. For more than 25 years, I have seen the fruit of a true father in the faith that has produced some of the greatest leaders in the Body of Christ. What a joy and honor it is to recommend *Authentic Spiritual Mentoring*.

BOB WEINER
President, Weiner Ministries International, Gainesville, Florida

Larry Kreider speaks directly on how to mentor people into their individual life callings. In a microwave society where we are accustomed to looking for heat-and-stir recipes, Larry takes us back to the Bible and builds a model that will produce lasting fruit.

MICHAEL P. FLETCHER
Manna Church, Fayetteville, North Carolina

This is by far the best book I have read on the subject of spiritual mentoring. Larry has lived these principles and has true authority and experience on this subject. Practice these principles and your ministry will be multiplied into many others and future generations.

JIM ORRED
Youth With A Mission, Kailua-Kona, Hawaii

What the Church needs today is for men and women to be spiritual parents. I found myself challenged by Larry's writing, touched by the stories, and filled with hope that the Church will arise to God's call to be spiritual fathers and mothers.

DOMINIC YEO
Trinity Christian Centre, Singapore

Once again, Larry Kreider has pioneered the way for others with this new book that combines experience, knowledge and passion to guide us into Kingdom community. Read it with a highlighter in your hand and a person you wish to mentor in your heart!

RALPH NEIGHBOUR
Touch Ministries, Houson, Texas

I loved the real-life illustrations Larry used to explain why believers are desperately in need of spiritual mentoring. Larry lays the biblical foundations for mentoring others and then teaches us how to do it. Thanks, Larry.

JOEL COMISKEY, PHD
Joel Comiskey Group, Moreno Valley, California

To my wife, LaVerne,
to my family
and to everyone who reads this book and
becomes a spiritual mentor.
May you find great joy in fulfilling
your call from God.

CONTENTS

PART I:
The Importance of Spiritual Mentoring

PART II:
Finding a Spiritual Mentor

PART III:
BEING A SPIRITUAL MENTOR

Acknowledgments

A very special thanks goes to Karen Ruiz, who does a superb job as my editor and writing assistant.

Thank you to those who gave valuable insight to this book: Sarah Sauder, Peter Bunton, Steve Prokopchak and Ron Myer.

And thanks to Gary Greig, Aly Hawkins and the entire Regal team. It is a joy to work with you!

PART I

THE IMPORTANCE OF
SPIRITUAL MENTORING

CHAPTER 1

WANTED:
SPIRITUAL MENTORS

 Key: Everyone is called to be a mentor.

Recently I spoke to a group of young people at one of America's dynamic mega churches, and a young man approached me after my session. "I'm on staff here, but I'm leaving next month," he confided.

I was puzzled. "Why?"

He looked deeply into my eyes. "Larry, if just one person in leadership in this church sat down with me for an hour once a month for a cup of coffee and asked me how I was doing, I would stay." He was looking for a spiritual mentor—someone to spend some time with him, someone who could offer support and guidance and feedback as he learned to use his gifts and talents within the Church. But everyone was too busy, and the many church programs had to go on.

A few years ago, I was traveling with a well-known evangelist in New Zealand, and he said something I will never forget. He turned to me with a tired, almost wistful note in his voice and said, "Larry, you know what I really need? I need a mentor." Here was a powerfully anointed leader, highly successful as an evangelist, whose greatest need was for someone who cared deeply to interact with him. He needed someone to act as a sound-ing board and to help him turn problems into opportunities. He was longing for a spiritual mentor—a seasoned Christian man to encourage him and give him advice and support.

Another time, a new Christian stopped by our house, de-pressed and discouraged. "LaVerne and Larry," she said to my wife and me, "I know the Lord has changed my life, but there is so much I don't understand. I'm not sure if I'll make it. I just can't decipher half of what I hear in church." Then she admit-ted the true cry of her heart: "I really need someone to help me understand the things that I'm taught. I need someone to help me grow up spiritually."

An elderly pastor I knew was ready to retire and hand the baton over to the younger leadership, but he had not trained up anyone to take his place. He nearly wept as he admitted that he had somehow missed the mark when it came to training and nurturing his spiritual protégés. They did not honor him or look to him as a mentor.

I hear stories like these again and again. As I travel through-out the world, training leaders and potential leaders week after week, I see a consistent and desperate need for spiritual men-tors who are willing to serve as spiritual fathers and mothers. Whether they are new believers, Christians for many years or even pastors, the need is still the same: Deep down inside, they are longing to be mentored. God has created us with a need to feel connected in relationships, but a painful lack of nurturing, support and interaction in the Church has created a void.

More and more believers are awakening to the need. A few years ago in our county in Pennsylvania, there was a powerful move of God among young people. It started when a few youth got serious about reaching their peers for Christ. The Bible study they started with a handful of kids grew to more than 1,000 attending every Tuesday night. One of the young leaders told me why he felt the Lord chose our area for a move of God: "We had spiritual fathers here who were ready and willing to serve and encourage us."

Because spiritual mentors poured what the Lord had given them into these young people, young leaders were produced who were prepared to become spiritual mentors themselves. The next generation felt well-loved and well-trained to pass on a lasting legacy of their own.

The Uncommon Individual Foundation, an organization devoted to mentoring research and training, reports that "mentoring is the third most powerful relationship for influencing human behavior, after marriage and the extended family."[1]

Randy MacFarland, who helps train mentors as Vice President of Training and Mentoring at Denver Seminary, says, "When we consider the fragmentation of the family, the speed of change demanding the constant learning of new skills, and our mobile society separating extended family members, the need for mentoring increases . . . we often forget how powerful it is when someone believes in us."[2] That's what mentors do: They believe in the younger generation. They help shape lives while passing on a legacy.

But what happens when a generation is left to its own resources and not provided with mentoring care?

PRESERVING LIVES: AN ILLUSTRATION

A few years ago I visited Pilanesberg Park, a South African game preserve, and learned that not too many years earlier the survival of the white rhinoceros in this game park was in question. Several of these endangered rhinos had been found slaughtered. The game wardens decided to electronically tag and track the remaining rhinos, placing video cameras in strategic locations to record any evidence of foul play.

After tracking the rhinos and reviewing the video footage, park officials were astounded to discover that young bull elephants were harassing the rhinos without any provocation. Although unnatural for them, these teenaged elephants were chasing the white rhinos for long distances and throwing sticks at them until they were exhausted, and then stomping them to death. Why were these young elephants acting so violently? The answer could be found in a decision made 20 years earlier.

At that time, park officials decided to transport some elephants from another national park into the Pilanesberg preserve because the other location was unable to support the increasing population. The elephants too large to transport were killed, including a number of mature bulls. Only younger elephants were sent to Pilanesberg, where they matured without the influence and presence of mature males. Park rangers and scientists discovered—through investigating the rhinos' mysterious deaths—that without the presence of mature bulls, these young male elephants were suffering from excessive aggression and becoming violent.

To remedy the situation and preserve the white rhino population, park officials killed five of the most aggressive young bull elephants and then imported older bulls in order to influence the remaining young males. The young bulls learned quickly that they were no match for the more mature elephants. The older bulls began to assume their place among the herd as fathers and disciplinarians.

Some park officials were surprised when it became apparent that the young bulls enjoyed these new relationships with the older, more mature males. The former lawbreakers returned to normal patterns of elephant behavior, and there were no reports of dead rhinos after the arrival of the mature elephants.

Looking for Real-Life Role Models

This story illustrates what younger Christians can gain if they have spiritual mentors to help them by supporting, counseling and teaching them. On the other hand, it also demonstrates what happens when seasoned Christians fail to act as spiritual mentors. When mature Christians neglect their responsibility to share their wisdom and love with younger Christians, the younger ones are not fully equipped for the task that lies ahead. They may be energetic and gifted, but without direction and loving oversight, they may get off track—or even trample those in their path.

There is a desperate need for spiritually mature men and women to mentor younger Christians, helping them to clarify what really matters in life and work. Spiritual mentors who act as mature coaches can help younger believers achieve their dreams and visions and feel connected as they integrate life and work and grow to maturity.

Instead of deep and nurturing relationships, too often in today's Church a believer is encouraged to participate in church services, Bible studies, para-church organizations or evangelistic ministries in order to bolster his or her faith and "grow strong in the Lord." The theory is that more teaching from God's Word plus more ministry participation equals more spiritual maturity. As important as these involvements may be, such a faulty supposition leads to believers inhaling message after message, book after book, CD after CD, seminar after seminar, all in order to fill a void for real relationship.

The result is a Christian who becomes fat spiritually and fails to interpret what he or she is learning so that he or she can pass it on to others. This person doesn't know how to meaningfully and sacrificially impart his or her life to others because he or she has never been properly parented. Without a role model, he or she remains a spiritual infant, needing to be spoon-fed by the pastor or other Christian worker.

But as God's people, we need to grow up. It is very difficult to do it by ourselves, just as natural infants cannot thrive if left on their own. Babies need the care and nurture of parents, just as believers need practical input from loving parents who delight when their children reach their full potential in Christ.

There are countless examples of spiritual mentoring or spiritual parenting in the Scriptures. Jesus modeled spiritual fatherhood to the 12 disciples. Paul discipled young Timothy. Elijah became a spiritual parent to Elisha. Moses trained Joshua to take his place to lead the children of Israel into the Promised Land. In all of these examples, the protégé was being prepared to stand in the place of his mentor to eventually fulfill God's greater purpose. In the case of Elijah and Elisha, the spiritual son even received an impartation of double anointing from his mentor (see 2 Kings 2:9-10). Throughout Scripture, we read about these one-on-one mentoring relationships and how they produce a rich legacy of impartation to future generations. We need this kind of connection and impartation today.

In the book *Connecting: The Mentoring Relationships You Need to Succeed in Life*, the authors begin their book with a surprising statement: "Research on biblical leaders led to a startling conclusion—few leaders finish well." They go on to say that in cases when leaders in the Bible did finish well, "their relationship to another person significantly enhanced their development."[3]

The apostle Paul knew that imparting a spiritual legacy should be his highest aim, and he was determined to finish well with strong relationships. He was a role model and spiritual father to many in the Early Church. He very clearly spelled out mentoring as his leadership model: "Follow my example, as I follow the example of Christ" (1 Cor. 11:1); "Whatever you have learned or received or heard from me, or seen in me—put it into practice" (Phil. 4:9). In other words, "Let me mentor you. Let me be your role model."

After a long absence from his spiritual children in the church at Thessalonica, Paul wrote a letter to them out of his concern that they might interpret his physical absence as proof he didn't care about them. He ended his letter by praying not only that God would direct his way back to them (see 1 Thess. 3:11), but also that they would love others in the same way that he loved them (see v. 12). He expected them to take up the loving responsibility of being spiritual parents for others. The New Testament Church was to model a growing and developing family. Every Christian was to become a spiritual parent!

CALLING ALL SPIRITUAL PARENTS

Apparently the church at Corinth needed some extra encouragement from Paul to take up the loving responsibility of becoming spiritual parents. Paul challenged the Corinthian church not to overlook this need: "For though you might have ten thousand instructors in Christ, yet you do not have many fathers . . ." (1 Cor. 4:15, *NKJV*).

Paul noticed that the Corinthian church had many teachers in their spiritual lives, but few spiritual mentors. Since the time Paul had brought them to faith in Christ, many instructors had taught God's Word to the Corinthians. They had heard these instructors and faithfully attended church services, but they then became arrogant in their knowledge of the gospel (see v. 18). They were proud of what they knew, but they were immature as believers. They lacked true parents or mentors to give them proper training and nurturing, to help them put their knowledge into life practice.

Paul knew that in order for the church to grow spiritually, each believer must be in vital relationships with others who had gone down this spiritual road before—otherwise they would be content to do what the "instructors" told them to do rather than learning how to hear from God themselves. This was wisdom that could only be learned as they received mentoring from a loving spiritual father. To jumpstart the process, Paul told the Corinthians that he was sending Timothy to "remind you of my way of life in Christ Jesus" (4:17). Paul had trained Timothy, his beloved and trustworthy spiritual son, and now Timothy would come to train them. Paul trusted Timothy to help the wayward Corinthian church because Paul had trained him like a son. Timothy was ready to impart *his* spiritual fatherhood to the Corinthian church. With Paul and Timothy's example, the Corinthian church would soon be producing their own spiritual sons and daughters. Paul was confident that when believers see spiritual fathering modeled, they are equipped to pass on a legacy to the next generation.

It was a lack of mature leadership in the Corinthian church that stunted the believers' spiritual growth. Unequipped to grow up spiritually, they struggled to find their identity in Christ. They did not know who they were in the Lord. Deficient of true spiritual fathers to model fatherhood, the Corinthian church had become a system that produced programs and teachers, not a family producing sons and daughters.

Because they did not have their identity grounded in Christ, the Corinthians sought it through their favorite leader: "I follow Paul . . . I follow Apollos . . ." (1 Cor. 3:4). Paul chided the Corinthian church for its lack of maturity, making it plain that while people have a role to play, it is clearly only God who is the source of any good thing and they should ultimately follow only Him. What they really needed were spiritual fathers and mothers to pay close attention to them so that they could be nudged toward maturity. They needed spiritual parents to sow into their lives, expecting them eventually to become spiritual parents themselves, creating a spiritual harvest of believers with Christ-grounded identities that would continue to multiply down through the generations.

God's intention is to produce spiritual parents who are willing to nurture spiritual children and help them grow into spiritual parents. This is a fulfillment of the Lord's promise to "turn the hearts of the fathers to the children, and the hearts of the children to their fathers" (Mal. 4:6). The Lord is restoring harmony among fathers and their children, both natural and spiritual, so that parents can freely impart their inheritance to the next generation. Children need parents who nurture strong character and assure them that they are valuable—that they are gifts from God. As children mature, they in turn must nurture the next generation.

Everyone is called to be a mentor: We are nurtured as children to become parents.

Chapter 2

Making a Spiritual Investment

 Key: Spiritual children are our inheritance.

Wouldn't it be great if someone saw your potential in Christ and decided to invest in your life? What do you think would happen if more Christians made themselves available in spiritual parenting relationships?

My friend Don Finto, who served as the senior pastor of Belmont Church in Nashville, Tennessee, for many years, has a great passion to father younger men in ministry. One of his more famous "spiritual sons," the singer and musician Michael W. Smith, says the effect on his life has been profound:

> I don't think I'd be where I am today if it hadn't been for Don. I've saved all his letters. He has encouraged me in so many ways—my self-confidence and who I am in the Lord—pulling stuff out of me that nobody ever was able to pull out. [1]

The potential for relationships such as Don and Michael's in today's Church is truly enormous. Geese fly in a "V" formation because the aerodynamics of the "V" enable the geese to fly over 70 percent farther than if they fly alone. As each bird flaps its wings, an updraft is created for the bird behind it. When the bird in front gets tired, he moves back in the formation. Geese go a lot farther when they work together. That is the point of a spiritual parenting relationship: We can go a lot farther spiritually when we work together in family-like units to reach the world.

Leaving a Spiritual Legacy

Have you ever heard of the Shakers? They were a religious group that flourished in the early nineteenth century that built large communities in the eastern United States. Because of their peculiar practice of trembling at their meetings, they were called "Shakers."

Today, the Shakers are history. The last and most visible trace of the group is the simple, well-made furniture they crafted. Why did this once-thriving group so rapidly die out? Because the Shakers believed in and practiced celibacy above marriage. They had little opportunity to multiply. Soon, even the religious revivals that brought many converts to Shakerism lost momentum, and the group declined in the late 1800s.

When we reproduce no children, our legacy is stunted and our posterity dies, very much like the Shakers. Without spiritual fathers and mothers to raise the next generation, we are in grave danger of dying out. All that's left will be religious furniture stuck in a corner somewhere, occasionally admired with a sense of nostalgia and regret.

My extended family gathers every year for a reunion—aunts, uncles, brothers, sisters, cousins, nephews and nieces who are all connected to the Kreider family tree. When my grandparents were alive, I noticed how they looked at each other with a twinkle in their eyes at these family gatherings. They knew we were all there because of them, and it gave them deep satisfaction to see their posterity.

The Lord wants to see spiritual families continually reproducing in each generation down through the ages. The apostle Paul was thinking in terms of *four* generations when he called Timothy his son and exhorted him to find faithful men to whom he could impart what Paul had taught him: "And the things you [second generation] have heard me [first generation] say in the presence of many witnesses entrust to reliable men [third generation] who will also be qualified to teach others [fourth generation]" (2 Tim. 2:2). Paul was thinking about his spiritual legacy and speaking as a spiritual father to his son, who would in turn give him spiritual grandchildren and great-grandchildren. The entire Bible was written from a family perspective. It was natural for Paul to think in terms of spiritual posterity because that is how biblical society was set up and the way God intended it to be. The Lord has a generational perspective and we must as well.

MULTIPLYING YOUR INHERITANCE

God has called us to become spiritual fathers and mothers in our generation. With this comes the expectation that our spiritual children will have their own spiritual children who will have even more spiritual children, thus providing ever-increasing multiplication.

Your inheritance will be all the spiritual children that you can someday present to Jesus Christ. No matter what you do—whether you are a housewife, a student, a worker in a factory, a pastor of a church, a missionary, or the head of a large corporation—you have the divine blessing and responsibility to birth spiritual children, grandchildren and great-grandchildren. You are called to impart to others the rich inheritance that God has promised.

While I was serving as a pastor, I was asked to minister at a training seminar to equip church leaders to become effective spiritual fathers and mothers. The seminar was at a four-year-old church in Lincoln, California, pastored by Daren Laws. I was amazed at what I experienced there. More than 80 percent of the people in the church were new believers. Even the mayor and his wife had come to faith in Christ. This fledgling church was already 600 people strong and was focused on training spiritual fathers and mothers to minister to young Christians. Daren and his team did not focus on church programs but instead on Jesus and on spiritual parenting.

When a person came to Christ, he or she was immediately invited to a home church (or small group). There the new Christian was connected by relationships into the Body of Christ. A spiritual parent nurtured the new believer until she could become a spiritual parent herself, and a new generation of believers was birthed! That church in California understands multiplying their inheritance.

I like how Abraham responded when the Lord showed him the stars in the heaven and promised him descendants as numerous as the stars: "And [Abraham] believed in the Lord . . ." (Gen. 15:6). What did he believe the Lord for? His inheritance! We, too, need to "believe the Lord" for many spiritual children. We can trust God to do it. It may not happen overnight, but it *will* happen when we trust in God's faithfulness and obey our calling to spiritual mentoring.

After ministering at a church in Dallas, Texas, a young man ran up to me holding a Bible and wanted to tell me his story:

> My folks are not Christians, but recently I opened up this Bible I found lying on the coffee table. After reading in it, I realized I needed Jesus. I gave my life to Christ and then drove around with my Bible in hand

looking for a church family. I found a church building near where I live and walked in.

The first person to greet me was a young lady, and after telling her my story, she called her father over and said, "Tell my dad what you told me."

The dad listened to my testimony with interest and then examined the Bible I held in my hands. "Fifteen years ago," he said, "I witnessed to a man I served with in the military. He declined to receive the Lord but agreed to take the Bible you are holding. The man I witnessed to was your father!"

The young Texan went on to tell me the rest of the story. He was now engaged to marry the young lady he met at the church building, and they were excited about serving as small-group leaders. The spiritual lineage begun by her father would continue. What an awesome story of spiritual posterity in God's kingdom!

FAMILIES MULTIPLY

The Lord wants us to be fruitful and multiply (see Gen. 1:28). Our God is a God of multiplication.

Multiplication is a fact of nature. As a farm boy, I once counted the kernels on a healthy stalk of corn and found there to be 1,200 kernels in the first generation. Consider this: If each of those kernels were planted, by the next generation there would be 1,440,000 kernels of corn! In the same way, healthy cells in the body multiply and result in growth of the body. A living cell is in a state of constant reproductive activity.

The Early Church documented in the book of Acts multiplied rapidly because they functioned in close relationship with each other, and this healthy activity and interdependence resulted in multiplication (see Acts 2:47). They understood the value of small groups in homes to aid in nurturing believers through spiritual family relationships.

As the Lord restores spiritual family life into His kingdom today, the Church will also multiply rapidly. We must be ready. We must properly train and prepare spiritual parents and sons and daughters so that Christ may be formed in them. Romans 8:19 says, "The creation waits in eager expectation for the sons of God to be revealed." When Christ is fully formed in His people, creation is going to sit up and take notice!

Paul was longing to see his spiritual children in Thessalonica when he wrote to them: "For what is our hope, our joy, or the crown in which we will glory in the presence of our Lord Jesus when he comes? Is it not you? Indeed, you are our glory and joy" (1 Thess. 2:19-20). The apostle had just told the Thessalonian believers that he was a spiritual father to them a few verses earlier (see vv. 7-11). Then he made clear that his spiritual children were his glory and joy—his inheritance! Paul rejoiced like a winner receiving a crown of victory at the games when he thought of the spiritual children and grandchildren he would present to Christ. He knew down to his bones that our spiritual sons, daughters and grandchildren are our spiritual posterity.

Several years ago I was in Barbados training church leaders and believers on the subject of spiritual parenting. The day I was to come back to the U.S., Bill Landis, a missionary who leads Youth With A Mission's Caribbean ministry, asked me to his home before going to the airport. Bill and his family, along with a team of leaders, were in the process of equipping Bajan Christians to become spiritual leaders. On this visit to his house, Bill told me some interesting history about this tiny island nation.

He explained that, years ago, many people in Barbados were brought as slaves to the island from West Africa, from places including the nation of Gambia. But now, Bill and his team are training Bajan Christians as missionaries so that they can return to their ancestral country of Gambia and lead Muslim Gambians to Christ. With a common heritage, it is the ideal match.

Then Bill said something that moved me deeply: "Larry, do you realize the people being reached in Gambia are a part of your spiritual heritage? You were one of my spiritual fathers, so you have a part in the ongoing legacy."

As I sat on the plane returning to the United States, I was dumbfounded at the significance of Bill's words. Years ago, long before I was a pastor or an author or a church leader, I was a young chicken farmer from Lancaster County, Pennsylvania, who led a Bible study of young people. During that time, I was a spiritual father to Bill.

Bill was a spiritual father to those Bajans he had discipled in Barbados. The Bajan Christians who were now going to Africa to lead Gambians to Christ were like my spiritual grand-children, and the spiritual children they birthed and nurtured in Gambia would be my great-grandchildren. Generations to come would receive God's promises because a chicken farmer had been obedient to God's call to disciple a bunch of rambunctious teenagers 30 years ago. Yes, this was part of my spiritual legacy. As I pondered this reality, I was deeply moved. I was the beneficiary of a large inheritance that had multiplied beyond my wildest dreams!

HARVEST TIME

We live in exciting days in the history of the Church. I believe we are on the verge of a great end-time harvest (see Rev. 7:9). Statistics show us that the ratio of people being saved today compared to 20 years ago is escalating. Clearly, the wind of the Holy Spirit is sweeping our world in an unprecedented manner! In the next years as we race toward the last chapter in history, we must prepare for hundreds of thousands of people who will come into the kingdom of God in our communities.

Jesus tells us to be constantly alert and ready: "Do you not say, 'Four months more and then the harvest'? I tell you, open your eyes and look at the fields! They are ripe for harvest" (John 4:35). I grew up on a farm. I know that various crops are ready to be harvested at different times of the year. We had to be alert, with our barns and equipment ready, so that we could harvest our crops at just the right time to reap a good harvest.

Down through the ages, the Lord has continually drawn people to Himself as many were harvested into His kingdom. Sometimes, however, a large portion of the harvest was lost because Christians were not alert and ready. It seems to me that one such huge harvest for which the Church was not prepared occurred in the late 1960s to mid-1970s. It was called the Jesus People movement. This harvest began when a number of believers in Christ entered the hippie counterculture community and shared the gospel of Jesus Christ with them, resulting in a massive number of conversions to Christianity among young people. By early 1971, there were Jesus People coffeehouses, communes and other enterprises in every state and province across the United States and Canada.

But much of the Church was unprepared for this radical new breed of Christians. The tension between the Jesus People and established churches was a source of irritation both for the Jesus People, who saw the Church as slow moving and steeped in tradition and legalism, and for the members of the institutional church, who often could not understand these kids with long hair and sandals. Although some churches and Christian communities did welcome these new converts with open arms and disciple them, many new believers fell by the wayside and became disillusioned until they were eventually lost to the Body of Christ.

If the Church had been prepared and had more under-standing of and compassion for those young people during that huge revival, I believe the harvest could have been much greater. In my opinion, there were simply not enough spiritu-al fathers and mothers willing to put their arms around these "Jesus freaks" and nurture them as babes in Christ until they could stand on their own. May we not make the same mistake in this generation!

The Lord is calling for thousands of spiritual fathers and mothers to prepare now for the coming harvest. I believe that mentoring is a God-designed development that is connected to the Great Commission, and that we must embrace it to realize the full potential of the great harvest. I believe that mentoring is an important part of a discipleship formation strategy of Jesus, and the investment in others will pay off great dividends of a multiplied spiritual inheritance.

Think about it: As a disciple-maker, you can influence countless others and impact the world as you make an invest-ment that keeps on growing. If you mentor one person who dis-ciples another, and that one person disciples yet another and those persons would each mentor one person, the multiplica-tion effects are astounding!

Are you ready to pour your resources into nurturing the spiritual strength of others? This kind of investment is done likely without thanks and without any immediate ROI (return on investment). But God promises that when you invest, lives are changed. You have the opportunity to make an investment in someone's life that will not only have a significant impact on the world—it will last through eternity!

CHAPTER 3

CALLED TO BE FAMILY

 Key: Mentoring involves family-type relationships as a way of life.

More than 30 years ago, as young youth workers, my wife, LaVerne, and I began to develop what we then called Paul-Timothy discipling relationships with new Christians. I met with a few young men each week for Bible study and prayer and LaVerne did the same with young women. Early on, we realized these relationships were going to be a work in progress, and it might be a long haul before we saw spectacular results. Many of the kids came from one particular neighborhood where gangs and drugs were problematic, and because most of the kids were first generation believers, they received little support from friends and family.

We were young ourselves—we didn't know much and made many mistakes, but our hearts were in the right place. After a short time, we knew that in order for these kids to grow spiritually and not fall away, we had to do more than spend time in a discipleship-type Bible study with them. They needed to see Christianity practically modeled and actually working or none of it would make any sense to them. We didn't call it mentoring or spiritual fathering at the time, but we were doing it just the same. It was more than a duty or event for us—it was a lifestyle of being connected in relationships to younger Christians who desperately needed supportive, nurturing commitment from older Christians.

We opened our hearts and home to these kids and loved them unconditionally. Deep down we realized (though we weren't looking very far ahead at the time) that if we coached them to grow up spiritually, they could someday help others . . . and that would make every minute invested worth the effort.

So we welcomed these teenagers into our daily lives. They spent a lot of time hanging out at our house, creating permanent red Kool-Aid stains on the carpet and punching occasional holes in the wall during wrestling matches. Most of the training took place as they observed us lovingly disciplining our children or doing laundry or fixing that persistent leak in the roof. We learned step by step—with fits and starts—how to be effective spiritual parents, and they learned how to bear fruit as Christians.

The Lord was faithful: Out of our modest beginnings, a church was eventually birthed with some of those young believers who hung around our house, and they were trained to take on the next batch of spiritual children. Today through DOVE Christian Fellowship International (DCFI), an international family of churches, we have the privilege of seeing many of our spiritual children, grandchildren and great-grandchildren reproduce spiritual sons and daughters as new small groups and dozens of new churches are planted throughout the world.

There was nothing special about us—and there still isn't! We were ordinary young people who made lots of mistakes. To be certain, we have many stories that are not success stories, but we had the heart of parents to teach our children. We loved Jesus, we really loved those kids and, just like any parent, we expected them to grow!

Research shows that children learn best from observing and imitating behavior that is modeled. A father models acceptable behavior for his children, *leading* rather than *driving* them. Modern sheepherders often drive their flocks with the help of dogs, but the shepherds of ancient Israel walked ahead and the sheep followed. God has revealed Himself to us as a Father and He is calling fathers and mothers to follow His leading. Spiritual parents, in turn, are to model Christlike behavior and attitudes as their children follow after.

A NOTE ABOUT GENDER AND AGE

In this chapter, we explore in-depth the common hallmarks of spiritual parents and the specific qualities brought to mentoring by men and women. But before we take a closer look at spiritual mothering and fathering, it should be mentioned that we believe men should mentor men and women should mentor women, as modeled in Titus 2: "That the older men be sober, reverent, sound in faith . . . likewise exhort the young men to be sober-minded . . . the older women likewise, that they be reverent in behavior . . . teachers of good things—that they admonish the young women to love their husbands . . ." (*NKJV*).

In counsel and example, the early Christian Church followed the mentoring method of older women with younger women and older men with younger men. There is a good reason for this. Fathering and mothering relationships fast become intimate friendships, and maintaining the boundaries of friendship between a man and a woman can be tricky. Deeply shared Christian love can be misinterpreted, leading to inappropriate emotional and physical attachments.

In my opinion, simply avoiding this trap is the best policy. "Abstain from all appearance of evil," says 1 Thessalonians 5:22 (*KJV*), or in my paraphrase, "Avoid anything that could appear to reflect sin rather than uprightness." I believe it is entirely appropriate, however, for a husband and wife team to mentor a spiritual son or daughter together. In Acts 18:24-26, we read about the husband and wife team of Aquila and Priscilla, who helped enlighten Apollos concerning his knowledge of the gospel. Priscilla and Aquila "explained to him the way of God more adequately" (v. 26).

In contrast to gender, chronological age does not dictate when someone can be a spiritual parent. You can be a spiritual mentor when you are 16 or 80. Between the ages of 12 and 16, all three of our daughters became spiritual mentors to younger girls in a small-group ministry. They took those kids under their wings and taught them simple biblical principles from God's Word. They prayed with them and cared for them when they had a need. Our daughters learned by *doing*. Out of their love for Jesus and those small girls, they took a step of obedience. They did not wait until they felt they were totally equipped; they became spiritual parents while they were learning themselves.

I was teaching at a seminar in Medford, Oregon. After the meeting, a young lady came up to me and thanked me for flying across the country to speak at her church. I asked her what the Lord was doing in her life. "Well," she said, "I have a few girls in school that I am meeting with each week to help them grow in their Christian lives." It was clear to me that she was a spiritual mother.

"How old are you?" I asked.

"Twelve," she replied. She was a spiritual mother at the age of 12! I meet many believers in their 50s and 60s who feel they cannot do what this 12-year-old has accepted as normal Christian living. What is wrong with this picture?

You can always find someone younger spiritually whom you can disciple and train in the ways of God—and soon they will be ready to train others, too. We need to learn how to release spiritual parents of all ages to reproduce. When the Bible exhorts older men to train younger men and older women to train younger women, it means that a spiritual parent should be a mature Christian who reflects *experience*. This does not necessarily mean an older-in-age woman needs to mentor a younger-in-age woman. *Age* has less to do with maturity than *experience*. Experience and spiritual maturity should be the yardstick that indicates who should mentor whom. Regardless of age, it is the person's spiritual maturity that qualifies him or her to mentor another.

That means that a Christian in his 20s who is spiritually mature may be a spiritual father to a 50-year-old man who is new to the Christian faith. Recently I met for breakfast with a medical doctor who came to faith in Christ in his 40s. He spoke endearingly of a spiritual father in his life, much younger in age, who helped him grow in his newly found faith.

This younger-in-age father and older son variation may be the exception, however. More often, I believe the biblical mandate of spiritual mothering and fathering normally follows the pattern of age. It is the older person with years of experience— the mature believer who has already been through many different seasons in life—who can more effectively mentor a younger person. Nevertheless, in both dynamics, the age differences work together to enrich the relationship.

Now let's explore how spiritual fathers and mothers mentor in different ways to bring maturity and vibrancy to the faith of their spiritual children.

FATHER FIGURE

"Family" has long been God's idea. He ordained and designed it: "I will be a Father to you, and you will be my sons and daughters, says the Lord Almighty" (2 Cor. 6:18). Paul the apostle's affectionate prayer for his beloved Ephesians was, "For this reason I kneel before the Father, from whom his whole family in heaven and on earth derives its name" (3:14-15). God is the Father of an entire great family, which includes all those who name Jesus Christ as Lord. He is the Father from whom all fatherhood derives its meaning and inspiration. We have to understand *His* Fatherhood—His love, forgiveness and acceptance—if we are to understand healthy family relationships.

Unfortunately, many in today's generation have a warped understanding of fatherhood because many fathers have abused their authority or been absent, causing a breach of trust and a lack of security. With poor role models in the world, God's people, the Church of Jesus Christ, must stand in the gap created by missing or cruel fathers to model God's intention for family.

"The church must begin to understand its role as a parenting influence—as a holistic life-growth community," says my friend Robert Stearns in his book *Prepare the Way*. This is what Stearns sees happening when we begin to understand that parenting role:

> God will lead many men who have the father's heart to begin to mentor young men in their congregations . . . older women will take younger under their wings and impart love, nurture and wisdom. Strong families will reach out to single-parent homes and welcome ongoing interaction between the families, bringing strength and combating the overwhelming sense of "aloneness." We will move toward the joy that the early church exuded as they lived in fellowship with each other and the Lord.[1]

What an incredible picture! And it will become reality when we realize that we can no longer live independently of each other. God wants to restore fathering and mothering to His kingdom, and it starts with His promise to be a Father to us. But for believers to experience true family life, fathers must assume their responsibility as spiritual parents.

Fathers bring strength, stability and balance to the family. A natural father is meant to be a protector, counselor and guide to his children so that they can grow up secure in their father's love and guidance. If they lack a healthy father role model, children cannot achieve their destiny. According to Dr. David Cannistraci, healthy fathering is essential to success at every level of society:

> Sociologists are now confirming that fathers not only play an indispensable role in the home, but also in the nation. Many of the problems we face in America today—drugs, welfare, teenage pregnancy—are directly related to the absence of fathers throughout the past several decades. . . . Spiritual fatherlessness is a weakness in the body of Christ today; a great vacuum has been created by the scarcity of godly fathering. Like society, the church is plagued with problems. We need the same kind of discipline and accountability a natural father brings to a natural family. We need wisdom and maturity, a firm hand to guide us, balance to preserve us and experience to comfort us.[2]

Statistics today show a society with an alarming trend toward the deterioration of the family. Marriages are failing, parents are absent—and children are paying the emotional, financial, physical and spiritual consequences. A popular view some years ago was that external forces, such as street crime, bad schools and economic stress, were the culprits of the crisis in family life. Today's critics challenge this view. The revised thinking is that it is the breakdown of families that feeds these and more social ills.

It is only as we reclaim the family that our society can in turn be healed. Ken Canfield says it this way:

While many voices are crying out that we need more government to protect our families, the church is responding to a different voice—the voice of a Father. God has revealed Himself as our Father, and He is calling fathers within the church to follow His example.[3]

Similarities Between a Spiritual and a Natural Father
"There are at least five similarities between a spiritual father and a natural father," according to Dr. David Cannistraci.[4] If we understand these functions, we can begin to follow the model of the Father, as well as nurture these characteristics in the next generation of spiritual mentors:

1. *Fathers demonstrate love.* The love relationship between a father and his son provides the ideal environment for training and developing the character and life of the son. Without love a son may grow but he cannot flourish. Fathers affirm their children and provide the gentle security of an unwavering commitment to their well-being.

2. *Fathers train and discipline.* Fathers take a powerful part in firmly directing and guiding their children into activities and attitudes that will prepare them for success. A true father accepts responsibility for his children. The biblical role of a father is to raise his children to a place of maturity and fruitfulness.

3. *Fathers provide.* To "provide" means to sustain and enrich. What does a spiritual father provide for his spiritual children? An inheritance of God's blessing. A legacy of spirit can only come from a spiritual father to his spiritual children.

4. *Fathers reproduce.* In the most basic sense, natural fathers are men who have physically contributed to creating a new life. Spiritual fathers give spiritual life to new children in the faith by becoming the vessels through which those children enter into new birth. They continue their ministries as fathers by raising up and reproducing their own ministries within those lives.

5. *Fathers bless and impart.* Many fathers understand well how to love, provide for and train their children, but many lack the ability that the great apostolic fathers of the Early Church profitably exercised: imparting spiritual blessing. The apostle Paul pictured God the Father blessing us as His children with all spiritual blessings through our relationship with Christ (see Eph. 1:3). Paul laid his hands on his spiritual son, Timothy, and was used to impart gifts and blessings that Timothy was responsible to utilize (see 2 Tim. 1:6). This transference of divine life is one of the most awesome responsibilities of a spiritual father. Speaking from experience, I can say that this is one of the greatest experiences any spiritual son can have.

Rebuilding Trust in Fathers

If the hearts of fathers are not restored to their children, both naturally and spiritually, Malachi 4:6 states that the Lord will "strike the earth with a curse." When relationships between the generations are estranged, they are—quite literally—cursed. God's desire is to take a generation that has been cursed by this breakdown of family relationships and to rebuild trust. The Son, Jesus, came to restore broken relationships—the relationship between the Father and mankind and the relationship between fathers and children. This family connection is a means for blessing and restoration between the generations.

Trust is often broken in today's society because parents have neglected their children at the expense of their own happiness or agendas. Children are left vulnerable in the wake of a divorce as they are shuttled between conflicting and sometimes hostile parents, and they often become frustrated, confused and insecure. This same kind of curse can exist between spiritual parents and their estranged spiritual children. Church leaders have often been so busy with their programs and committees that they have no time to train spiritual children to become future spiritual parents. This is a blight on the Church, stunting future generations of leaders.

I've heard it said that children should forgive their parents for being less than perfect, and parents should work hard to make sure their children have as little to forgive as possible. If the damage has already been done, both natural and spiritual children must reach a place of maturity where they can forgive their neglectful parents, or they will grow up angry and distrustful.

Our God wants to convict natural and spiritual fathers who have been irresponsible and caught up in their own agendas, of their neglect. He alone is the one who can repair the damage and reconnect fathers to their lonely children. Fathers must repent of their self-seeking and carelessness, and begin the long process of rebuilding their children's trust. The Lord wants to restore relationships between the young and the old so that a powerful spiritual legacy can persevere and proliferate.

MOTHER LOVE

One day, nine-year-old Joey got off the bus from school and said, "Mom, the bus is so empty that we each could have our own seat . . . but those dumb girls all pile into one!" Joey's maleness could not comprehend the females' need to cluster.

God created men and women unique with respect to one another. The differences between men and women are meant to be a blessing and bring balance to life so that we can have a richer and fuller comprehension of the Father's love for us. Women seem to be programmed for intimacy and deep friendships. Feminine traits are often described as soft, nurturing, intuitive and empathic. When women get together, they often talk about their feelings and relationships, their work and their families, and their nurturing, mothering characteristics often come out as they communicate with each other. Women see themselves in relation to the people around them, preferring intimacy to separateness. This allows women to be uniquely in tune with close relationships.

The nurturing tendency in women is most evident in their capacity for love, which often goes beyond that of men. In Proverbs 10:1, the author states, "A wise son brings joy to his father, but a foolish son grief to his mother." A mother usually feels deeper pain because her love for her children is more tender even than the father's.

Of course, you don't have to be a biological mother to display tenderness and compassion. Any Christian woman who understands the heart of God and His everlasting love will develop nurturing, maternal characteristics. How do we know God has a tender, nurturing mother's heart? Passages such as Isaiah 49:15 and 66:13 describe how God loves His people as a mother loves her children. These passages demonstrate God's tenderness and desire to nurture us and make us fruitful.

Time and time again in the holy Scriptures we get a picture of God's nurturing, mother-like tendencies: "Can a mother forget the baby at her breast and have no compassion on the child she has borne? Though she may forget, I will not forget you! See, I have engraved you on the palms of my hands . . ." (Isa. 49:15). A little later in Isaiah the Lord says, "As a mother comforts her child, so will I comfort you" (66:13). God's deep, abiding love for us is greater than even that strongest of bonds between a baby and his mother.

Another picture of God's nurturing and tender mother's heart is found in Matthew 23, when Christ showed His compassion for those who rejected Him:

> O Jerusalem, Jerusalem, you who kill the prophets and stone those sent to you, how often I have longed to gather your children together, as a hen gathers her chicks under her wings, but you were not willing (v. 37).

Jesus longed to bestow His wonderful grace and favor to these spiritually blinded religious leaders in Jerusalem. Even though they refused His love, it was compassionately extended to them just as a mother hen gathers her chicks for protection, safety, warmth and comfort under her wings.

The Titus 2 Mandate

As a young, 28-year-old pastor's wife, LaVerne (my wife) struggled in the early days of ministry because of the pressure she felt to conform to the expected pastor's-wife role of organizing women's groups, meetings and programs. As she tells it, "I knew I was not going to be the typical pastor's wife who played the piano, organ or sang. I just did not feel called to be a public person. I knew God did not call me to spend my time heading committees and planning women's events. Every time I got down on my knees, I knew what God had called me to do. It was clear: Train a few women at a time."

So LaVerne spent the next few years doing just that. She started to pour her life into a few of the women who were small-group leaders in the church. It wasn't a job for the faint-hearted! The relationships she developed took time and effort. She was not standing up front, basking in the applause of an adoring public.

For years, she trained women behind the scenes. She loved them as she inquired how their marriages were faring. She prayed and wept with them as they went through life's hard spots and rejoiced with them when they experienced life's joys. Those women were equipped to pass on to other women the impartation they had received from LaVerne. The results have been a multiplication over and over again of LaVerne's initial efforts with a few women.

Today, LaVerne continues to mentor women one on one. When she speaks to larger crowds, young women frequently cry out, "But where are the older women? Where is that spiritual mother who will mentor me and help me grow up in my Christian life?" With tears streaming down their faces, younger women say, "Sometimes I could just use an hour of a spiritually mature woman's time. I so desperately need to be encouraged to look to the Father. I need to hear from someone who has spiritual maturity beyond mine and can teach me valuable lessons from her own experience. I need someone to tell me I am going to make it during this season of my life—that I'll make it to the end of the week!" Women are looking for a friend, a coach, a cheerleader who can point them to Jesus.

I believe the Lord is calling spiritual mothers to obey His call today to take spiritual daughters under their wings. Christian women need spiritual mothers to help them grow into healthy women of God. A spiritual mother walks alongside another woman, puts her arm around her and says, "You can make it!" In her book *Spiritual Mothering*, Susan Hunt writes that spiritual mothering is "when a woman possessing faith and spiritual maturity enters into a nurturing relationship with a younger woman in order to encourage and equip her to live for God's glory."[5]

God's Word gives women a clear mandate and model for spiritual mothering. Paul told Titus how to set up spiritual parenting relationships, and into this context he exhorted older women to put their energies into training and teaching younger women:

> [Teach] the older women . . . that they be reverent in behavior, not slanderers, not given to much wine, teachers of good things—that they admonish the younger women to love their husbands, to love their children, to be discreet, chaste, homemakers, good, obedient to their husbands, that the word of God may not be blasphemed (Titus 2:3-5, *NKJV*).

Paul knew the Church would be impacted if older women would start teaching younger women by their godly lifestyles. If mature women will give of themselves and invest their energies in younger women, the Kingdom will be advanced. God wants to use women of reverence (who fear God), who are free from slander and who are not captive to addictive behavior. These mature women are ready to be spiritual mothers.

Spiritually mature women unselfishly give of themselves. They submit their will to God and to His leadership. Out of love for Him, they have learned the secret of Philippians 2:3-4: "Let nothing be done through selfish ambition or conceit, but in lowliness of mind let each esteem others better than [herself]. Let each of you look out not only for [her] own interests, but also for the interests of others" (*NKJV*). Spiritually mature women are not absorbed by their own concerns but unselfishly look out for others.

The Challenge of Spiritual Mothering

Remember that it is the character of Christ that qualifies an individual to be a spiritual mother. Potential spiritual mothers must be women who fear God. This means they need to care more about what God thinks of them than what other people think. Suffering from a poor self-image will hinder spiritual mothering. There are pressures in life to conform and act a certain way, but when the fear of God comes over a woman, she asks God what *He* thinks of her. She knows Christ accepts her because of His blood, and that His is an unconditional love. This brings freedom into her life.

LaVerne was speaking at a women's retreat about God's unconditional love, and a woman who had been a Christian for a long time came up to her and said, "I don't think I understand God's unconditional love. Growing up, I felt love from my parents only when I performed satisfactorily for them. So I've always put conditions on my love when I related to others." That day, she acknowledged her wrong thinking and chose to accept God's unfathomable, unconditional love for her. Her life was changed! God loves individuals whether they perform or not. His love is extended without conditions. When God's people understand this, they will not minister to others out of duty, but out of His love for them. It is through this love that we serve one another (see Gal. 5:13).

Another thing that will hinder spiritual mothering is selfishness. "I'm too busy," "I've raised my children," "I'm retired . . . just let me relax by the ocean" are all selfish excuses for not investing in the growth of a spiritual daughter. Several years ago, at 48 years of age and after raising 7 children of her own, one of LaVerne's spiritual mothers, Naomi, took in a young foster son. Then her elderly mother moved in with her family. Some would look at Naomi and say, "Isn't it time to take a break and ease up?" But this dedicated mentor still found time to get together with LaVerne (she had to get a babysitter for her son and elderly mother at home) to pray with her.

And her commitment has made a lasting impression: "When I feel lazy and want to gripe and complain," says LaVerne, "I just can't make excuses for myself because I have a spiritual mom in my life who doesn't have it easy but chooses to walk in joy."

It takes a special kind of grace to be a natural or spiritual mother in today's world. Being a mother is not easy. There is a huge mental investment, along with the physical exertion of the 24-hours-a-day demand required for motherhood. A woman who understands this is willing to admit her total dependence on the grace of the Lord.

Although it is important to have loving and nurturing one-on-one relationships, these relationships must hinge on the more important vertical relationship with God. A spiritual mother-daughter relationship needs to focus on glorifying God and yielding to His will and purpose. A plaque in a mother's kitchen reads, "The greatest thing a mother can do for her children is to love their father." You could paraphrase that adage to say, "The greatest thing a spiritual mother can do for her spiritual children is to love her heavenly Father!" The entire focus of the relationship must be one of glorifying God.

This point is brought out clearly in the first chapter of Luke, where we witness the interaction between Elizabeth and Mary. Elizabeth and Mary had a lot in common: For one, they both had unusual pregnancies! When Mary came to visit Elizabeth, they could have focused on their unique situations and talked of all they were feeling, empathizing with each other and calling attention to their own needs. Instead, upon greeting each other, their focus was *upward*. Their relationship was not based on what they needed from each other. Elizabeth, like a seasoned spiritual mother, encouraged Mary, who, in turn, burst forth in praise to God:

And it happened, when Elizabeth heard the greeting of Mary, that the babe leaped in her womb; and Elizabeth was filled with the Holy Spirit. Then she spoke out with a loud voice and said, "Blessed are you among women, and blessed is the fruit of your womb! But why is this granted to me, that the mother of my Lord should come to me? For indeed, as soon as the voice of your greeting sounded in my ears, the babe leaped in my womb for joy. Blessed is she who believed, for there will be a fulfillment of those things which were told her from the Lord."

And Mary said: "My soul magnifies the Lord, and my spirit has rejoiced in God my Savior. For He has regarded the lowly state of His maidservant; For behold, henceforth all generations will call me blessed. For He who is mighty has done great things for me, and holy is His name" (Luke 1:41-49, *NKJV*).

The purpose of a spiritual mothering relationship is to glorify God. He is your hope: "Christ in you, the hope of glory" (Col. 1:27). What an awesome concept: Christ, the anointed One, lives within you! It is Christ who ministers through you. It's not about what you do for God, but about what God does in and through you. *He* does the spiritual mothering through you as you yield to Him.

DIFFERENCES OF MEN AND WOMEN IN SPIRITUAL PARENTING

Why is it that women trust other women so much more readily than men trust other men? How can women enter a room and almost immediately begin to open up and be vulnerable about their lives and their families while the men are opening up about last night's game or last week's fishing expedition? Do women respond differently to mentoring than men? I propose that there needs to be no difference, but, yes, most women seem to easily form relationships that lend themselves to deep mentoring, while most men struggle to do so. It's not wrong, simply different.

Women seem to be created to naturally gravitate toward the vulnerability that a mentoring relationship is built on. It takes a little more convincing for men. Men need to see a worthwhile purpose, a beginning and end, a goal to shoot for and a response from the one receiving our gift of time. Men want to know that this relationship is making a difference and has tangible, measurable results. They have adapted to certain rules in relationships and these rules are hard to breach. A few of these are: Don't trust unless the relationship has proven trustworthy. Don't be too vulnerable too soon. Watch for the level of energy expended in this relationship as compared to the results observed. Watch your level of personal involvement (that is, don't care too much).

While men are hungry for friendship, psychologist Dr. Ken Druck says, "We will not allow ourselves to get together with male friends because we enjoy their company. It is not 'safe' simply to want some male companionship. We have to legitimize the feeling. We have to throw in a card game, a ball game, or some beer to make the occasion a 'safe' one."[6]

Spiritual fathers and mothers must come to peace with who they are. To be a spiritual parent or mentor is not based on what the mentor needs. Too often we gravitate to what we feel we should be receiving, but this approach will skew the relationship from the starting blocks. Men, we must put to rest our preconceived ideas about the personal gains or benefits from our spiritual children. The reward is mostly eternal and yet even that "personal gain" must be far from our minds.

There are many times the mentoring relationship may feel, and in fact is, one-sided. After all, why not? As the mentor, I am responsible to be the initiator: the initiator of the phone calls, the initiator of the get-togethers, the initiator of prayer, the initiator of studying a book or the Bible. I am the initiator. There is no room for thoughts such as, "I called him last time" or "If he cared about this relationship, he would pay for breakfast."

I am not asking men to respond to mentoring like most women do, but I think it is important to identify some of the hurdles that men will undoubtedly face in this type of relationship. The goal is not to become feminized but to become like Jesus, who was the all-time best mentor who ever walked the earth. If Jesus was capable of transcending His maleness and closely connect with His disciples, then so can we. (More about The Jesus Model of mentoring in chapter 9.)

The heavenly Father made men and women differently and declared of those differences, "It is good." The truth is, we need both genders to rise to their full potential to parent more and more generations of healthy spiritual children. Let's look closer at how spiritual parents raise their children through mentoring.

WHAT PARENTS DO FOR THEIR CHILDREN

Before you can be a spiritual father or mother, you must first check your motives. Spiritual parenting is a behind-the-scenes kind of deal. It's not likely that someone will pat you on the back and say, "What a good job you are doing—keep up the good work!" Why? Because being a parent is not something you *do* as much as it is someone you *are*. I don't have to tell people I'm a father. They know it when they meet my son and my three daughters.

Scripture warns us about giving ourselves an impressive title in an effort to try to gain the honor and respect of others: "And do not call anyone on earth 'father,' for you have one Father, and he is in heaven. . . . The greatest among you will be your servant" (Matt. 23:9,11). The apostle Paul called himself a father several times in Scripture, but he used the word "father" to denote "not *authority*, but *affection*: therefore he calls them not his *obliged*, but his *beloved*, sons" (see 1 Cor. 4:14).[7] The measure of the greatness of a spiritual father is always the measure of his servanthood and love.

Let's explore what a spiritual mentor generally does.

Parents Love and Encourage Their Children

A spiritual parent loves and gently encourages her children to move in the right direction as they progress on their journey. The apostle Paul showed how much he loved the Thessalonian believers as a spiritual parent in his letter to them: "But we were gentle among you, like a mother caring for her little children. We loved you so much that we were delighted to share with you not only the gospel of God but our lives as well, because you had become so dear to us" (1 Thess. 2:7-8). Paul cherished the people he had mentored like a nursing mother, tender and gentle. When spiritual children are impacted with a parent's affection, they know it and respond.

With a mature spiritual parent at their side, children will grow strong and learn quickly and naturally by example. A parent teaches, trains, sets a good example and provides a role model. A spiritual parent raises a son's or daughter's awareness of attitudes or behaviors in their lives that need to be changed. He or she helps them take an honest look at their lives and make adjustments so that their actions and behavior can change. It's only when a spiritual child knows he is loved and accepted that he has the confidence he needs to make changes and hard choices.

Parents Expect Their Children to Grow

Parents expect their children to grow up in every way—physically, spiritually, mentally and emotionally. Through the natural progression of time, and with much love and the right amount of training, children are expected to mature into healthy adults and move out to start homes of their own.

Twenty-one years after having our first child, I walked down the aisle with my "baby" girl at my side on her wedding day. I realized I had spent all those years of time, effort and money just to give her away to her fiancé! We raised her to give her away. She and her husband now have three children of their own, and they have the opportunity to be parents and prepare the next generation. Parenting is all about passing on a legacy. Spiritual parenting involves a whole package of loving, training, modeling, imparting and multiplying—all with the expectation that your children will grow up to begin the cycle again.

In the book of Colossians, we read about how Paul modeled fatherhood to Epaphras when he made himself available in a time of need. It seems that Epaphras had been converted and carried the gospel to Colosse. Because of his previous relationship to Paul, Epaphras came to Rome to seek Paul's seasoned counsel about the errors that then threatened the Colossian church. In response, Paul wrote his letter, a letter from a father who cared deeply. Paul could write this fathering letter because he felt a stewardship for the people through his relationship with Epaphras (see Col. 1:7-8). Parents who model parenthood like this perpetuate a legacy through their sons and daughters as they, in turn, learn how to parent others into the Kingdom.

My friend and author Peter Bunton has years of experience training and mentoring young people. He has this to say about nurturing spiritual children to maturity: "A spiritual father or mother should be prepared to father or mother those of different personalities and gifts. Sometimes a very different mentor is needed to help spiritual sons or daughters learn other facets of their ministry. A test of a spiritual father's security is whether he can help someone more gifted than himself!"

I agree with Peter. It is a common desire of natural parents to see greatness in their children, a greatness that will make God's world a better place. Likewise, a spiritual parent should expect and desire his or her spiritual children to go far beyond him or her spiritually. Whether the spiritual child already has many gifts or receives a new impartation through the parent's example, it should be a mentor's greatest joy to see his or her children succeed.

Parents Set an Example for Their Children

In order to grow in God, people need someone to speak truth into their lives and model what it means to walk in faith. "Remember your leaders, who spoke the word of God to you. Consider the outcome of their way of life and imitate their faith" (Heb. 13:7). If mentors present a true and godly example to those they serve, their protégés gladly imitate them. This initiates a legacy of spiritual parenting.

In 1 Thessalonians 2:11, Paul reminds the church that he set an example as a father, exhorting, comforting and charging each believer "as a father deals with his own children." Spiritual mentors are models to emulate so that younger Christians can grow up to be nurturing, caring and encouraging adults and eventually capable, healthy parents themselves. It's no secret that children reared in healthy, loving families grow up to be healthy, loving parents. Providing an example for others to imitate and reproduce is an important aspect of spiritual parenting.

Parents Give Children a Sense of Significance

One goal of a parent is to build a healthy sense of self-worth in his daughter or son. In his book *Seven Things Children Need*, John

Drescher says that every child wants to be noticed and recognized as a person of worth:

> It is almost impossible to live with ourselves if we feel we are of little value or if we don't like ourselves. . . . A person who feels like a nobody will contribute little to life. This needs to be stressed because the great plague of inferiority feelings starts early in life. We human beings need to be noticed, appreciated, and loved as we are if we are to have a sense of significance.[8]

A few years ago, a young Dutch church planter named Bert told me how grateful he was for the spiritual fathers and mothers who believed in him and his wife, greatly impacting their lives on the mission field. "Spiritual mentors work to build a Christ-esteem in us so that our identity, security, self-esteem, value and destiny are built in Christ," he emphasized.

Leaders often become leaders only when someone believes in them as leaders. Years ago, there was a young believer in our small group who felt like he could not pray in public. Keith admitted he felt inadequate among all the more mature Christians whose prayers came easily. I did not give him a formula to follow, but I saw potential in him and encouraged him to step out of his comfort zone. One day, Keith urged me, "Ask me to pray sometime when I'm not expecting it." I was happy to oblige! Very soon at a small-group meeting, I asked Keith to begin our prayer session with a one-sentence prayer. It was a place to start, and Keith prayed because I believed he could do it. My trust in him helped him to overcome his feelings of inadequacy. He went on to assume leadership in a small group and later served as a deacon in his local church.

Spiritual children will grow in responsibility and achievement when someone believes in them. Parents must see their children in the light of who they can become.

Parents Offer a Place of Safety for Their Children

God wants to provide relationships where spiritual fathers and mothers contribute a sense of protection to their spiritual children so that they can mature in their Christian lives. As parents, we want to protect our natural children from the madness around them. We want them to know that however terrible the world becomes, they can find comfort and shelter in a God who cares deeply for them and wants them to take risks and succeed.

In the same way, spiritual children must feel safe to make mistakes and to take shelter from the world's ills. Spiritual children need protection, nurturing, care, guidance and encouragement from their parents.

SPIRITUAL PARENT: A DEFINITION

Spiritual fathers and mothers might be called *mentors* or *coaches* because they help sons and daughters negotiate the obstacles of their spiritual journeys. A coach is someone who wants to see you win. A coach tells you that you *can* make it. Simply stated, my favorite definition of a spiritual parent is:

> *A spiritual father or mother helps a spiritual son or daughter reach his or her God-given potential.*

It is that uncomplicated and that profound. Bobb Biehl says it this way: "Mentoring is more 'how can I help you?' than 'what should I teach you?'"[9]

Of course, spiritual parents *do* teach spiritual truths, but their energies often go more into caring for and helping the son or daughter in the many different aspects of his or her life. A spiritual parenting relationship cannot be a formal relationship of teaching because by definition and by practice, parenthood is informal interaction. It takes place along the highways and byways of life. Parenthood is a lifestyle.

HOW SPIRITUAL CHILDREN BECOME PARENTS

 Key: The three stages of growth for every believer

Somehow many of us have been duped into thinking that spiritual maturity can be attained only by super-saints who pray five hours a day, attend church four times a week and follow a vigorous Bible-reading program. And we despair when we don't measure up. While it is true that as we mature spiritually we will find ourselves wanting to read the Bible more often and pray more frequently, growing to maturity happens in much more practical and gradual ways. I believe growth happens especially as we reach out to the less spiritually mature rather than constantly needing to be fed ourselves. Maturity requires that we become more responsible for others.

Growing from a spiritual baby into a spiritual parent is crucial to God's divine order. That's why God established a natural training ground for us, consisting of "growth stages" through which we grow to parenthood. According to the Bible, these three growth stages are *child, young man* (or *woman*) and *father* (or *mother*). At each point in our journey, we function in a particular way and have distinct tasks to perform. John addresses all three spiritual stages in 1 John 2:12-14:

I write to you, dear children, because your sins have been forgiven on account of his name. I write to you, fathers, because you have known him who is from the beginning. I write to you, young men, because you have overcome the evil one. I write to you, dear children, because you have known the Father. I write to you, fathers, because you have known him who is from the beginning. I write to you, young men, because you are strong, and the word of God lives in you, and you have overcome the evil one.

International speaker, teacher and spiritual father Alan Vincent from San Antonio, Texas, has this to say about these verses in 1 John: "The cry of the apostle John was not only for strong men who knew the Word of God and could overcome the evil one, but for *fathers* who really knew God and who would come forth to father the church. If men as a whole became strong fathers according to the biblical pattern—in home, church and society—then most of our social problems would disappear and Satan's kingdom would be severely curtailed. Fatherhood is the foundation on which God has chosen to build the whole structure of society."

Children must grow up. They become spiritual young men and women by having the Word of God living in them and by overcoming the assaults of the devil. In turn, as young men and women grow into maturity and develop an intimate relationship with God, they become spiritual fathers and mothers—and in order to become spiritual parents, they need to have spiritual children!

If we fail to take the natural steps to becoming spiritual young men and women and then to becoming spiritual parents, we remain babies—spiritually immature and lacking parenting skills. It is sad, but this scenario is often the case in the Church.

Many times there are no provisions within our church systems to help believers develop and mature. Sometimes people simply do not want to take the responsibility to become a spiritual parent. They may feel they are too busy or will be burned out by a protégé. They may feel that they have little to offer because they don't feel mature enough themselves. Whatever the reason, I believe it is still God's best for everyone to be given the opportunity to do the work of ministry and connect in vital relationships with others. Through modeling and impartation, spiritual reproduction happens.

Let's take a look at how a spiritual child develops into a spiritual parent.

Spiritual Children

Natural babies bring new life to a family! They laugh and cry, expressing their needs immediately and freely. They are self-centered—they do not know any better, and we gladly supply their needs. Parents don't mind when babies mess in their diapers because that's what babies do. Although their fussing and crying may interfere with the parents' schedules, Dad and Mom are happy to care for their child because he is little and defenseless and needs help. Caring parents would never deny a child their attention.

Spiritual babies in the Body of Christ are wonderful, too! And good spiritual parents are happy to spend extra time with spiritual children in order to steer them in the right direction. They need constant assurance and care and often do the unexpected because they are still learning what it means to follow Jesus. According to 1 John 2:12, they are "children whose sins are forgiven," which puts them in fellowship with God and other believers. And that's their focus: forgiveness of sins, getting to heaven and learning to know the Father. Like natural babies, they know their Father, though it is probably not a thorough knowledge of God. Spiritual children are most aware of and alive to what they can receive from the One who saved them. They freely ask the Father when they have a need. Have you ever noticed how new believers can pray prayers that seem theologically unsound, yet God answers almost every one? The Father is quick to take care of these little ones.

But what happens when spiritual babies do not grow up? When men and women still have childish emotions, toddler angers and adolescent behaviors well into their adult years, psychologists call it *arrested development*. Those whose development is arrested have simply stopped growing emotionally and are stuck in an immature stage in life. And let's be honest: However endearing children are when they are young, childishness quickly loses its appeal if it does not pass with time. A childish adult is not attractive. Neither is a believer who has not grown up spiritually.

A pastor friend of mine lamented, "Sometimes I feel like I have to walk down the aisles each Sunday to give everyone their spiritual bottles. And what really bothers me is that I have to part the whiskers of some of the spiritual babies to give them their bottles!" In other words, it's not only new believers who are spiritual babies in the Church today. Older Christians who lack spiritual maturity are adults in age but babies in spiritual growth. They may be 20, 40, 60 or more years of age—believers for many years—and never have spiritually matured. They live self-centered lifestyles, complaining and fussing and throwing temper-tantrums when things don't go their way. Some do not accept the fact that God loves them for who they are. Others may wallow in self-pity when they fail. Still others may live under an immense cloud of guilt and condemnation.

The story is told of a little boy named Matthew whose mother put him to bed one night. About 30 minutes later she

heard a thump on the floor. She knew exactly what happened—
he had fallen out of bed. She went upstairs and Matthew was
sitting in the middle of the floor, looking bewildered. She
asked, "Matthew, what happened?"

He said, "I don't know. I guess I just stayed too close to where
I got in."

There are spiritual children who have stayed too close to
where they got in. They desperately need to grow up so that
they can become spiritual young men and women and eventually spiritual parents.

Parenting Spiritual Children

A new believer often acts like a natural child, with all the marks
of immaturity, including instability and gullibility. Like natural babies, they may be self-centered, selfish and irresponsible—
but spiritual parents know that eventually the children will
grow up. In time, they will mature as they grow into a loving
relationship with Jesus Christ. Good spiritual parents focus on
teaching the early lessons of Christian faith and moving their
children on to new horizons. They know that a growing person
is one who constantly reaches out for maturity in personhood
and personality.

To move their spiritual children on to the next stage of
maturity, mentors should:

- Teach them the Word of God either one on one or in
  a small-group setting where everyone is learning the
  same basic foundational teachings. (I suggest using
  the 12-book Biblical Foundation Series that I have
  written for this purpose.[1])

- Realize that new believers need more care than those
  who are more spiritually mature. In the same way you

place a stake next to a growing tree to give it stability and support as it begins to grow, new believers need the stake of a mature believer to stand with them as they begin their new life in Christ.

· Get the new believer involved with other believers in both a small group and larger group settings so that they do not become emotionally dependent on their mentors.

· Take their spiritual children with them as they live their lives before them. Mentors could take their spiritual children to the store with them or watch a football game with them. They should allow their spiritual children to see them in real-life situations.

SPIRITUAL YOUNG MEN AND WOMEN

Spiritual babies need to be spoon-fed, but young men and women have learned to feed themselves as they meditate on the Word of God. They have grown to the next stage, but they still have some growing up to do. Whether they are "young adults" in *chronological age* or *spiritual age*, they are not yet mature enough to mentor others; however, they are developing, and their youthful enthusiasm and idealism is a potent force. Young adults are often able to see the simple truth of a complicated matter and are able to work tirelessly for a good cause. Fearless and strong, they bring zeal to the Body of Christ.

According to 1 John 2:14, young men and women are strong with God's Word in their hearts, and they have won their struggle against Satan. They don't need to run to others in the Church to care for them like babies do, because they have learned how to apply the Word to their own lives. When the devil tempts them, they know what to do to overcome him. They use the Word of God effectively and powerfully!

Paul gives this advice to Timothy, his young friend and spiritual son: "Don't let anyone look down on you because you are young, but set an example for the believers in speech, in life, in love, in faith and in purity" (1 Tim. 4:12). Timothy was young in age, but Paul mentored him until he determined that he was spiritually mature and ready to be a spiritual father in his own right. Like Timothy, spiritual young men and women are strong in the Word and Spirit. They have learned to use the strengths of spiritual discipline, of prayer and of the study of the Word. They are alive to what they can do for Jesus, and one day soon, under the guidance of their mentors, they will be spiritual parents.

On the other hand, the temptations of youth may be a trap for those who have not yet developed a strong sense of right and wrong. Paul knew that Timothy, as a young person in age, was subject to the same passions as other young people. He warned him to "run from anything that gives you the evil thoughts that young men often have . . ." (2 Tim. 2:22, *TLB*). Spiritual young men and women must be cautioned to run from youthful passions that could lead to sin.

When I was eight years old, I thought my daddy knew everything. When I turned 13, I thought, "There are a couple of things this man doesn't know!" When I got to 16 years of age, there were times when I thought, "My father is prehistoric!" Then in my early 20s I got married, and a few years later we had our first child. I was shocked to discover all my father had learned in the last few years!

You know what happened—*I* was the one who had changed. I had matured and realized my dad knew much more than I thought he did. Parenthood had tempered me. Today I think of my father as one of the wisest men I know.

A young man or woman can easily become arrogant and dogmatic. After returning from Bible college or a short-term missions experience, or after having read the latest book, they may think they have all the answers. They are not yet tempered by parenthood. It's only by becoming spiritual fathers and mothers that they can be tempered, by really experiencing spiritual parenthood's joys and disciplines.

Spiritual parents must do everything they can to encourage young men and women to develop their ministries while they are still young, to become spiritual parents as soon as they are ready. To do so, mentors should:

- Give them small areas of spiritual responsibility. Ask them if they are comfortable to lead in prayer in a small group.

- If someone is sick and needs prayer, mentors should ask them to participate by praying a short prayer of faith along with them as they pray for healing for that person.

- If mentors meet with a small group for breakfast or for a cup of coffee and cannot be there, they should ask their spiritual son or daughter to organize this time of fellowship without them for a time or two.

- Ask them to pray daily for someone in their small group or local church so that they develop and grow spiritually.

- Encourage them to share, with both believers and unbelievers, their "God Story," describing how they came to faith.

SPIRITUAL FATHERS AND MOTHERS

Susan, a young mother and a new believer, joined one of her church's small groups, expecting to learn biblical values and spend time with fellow Christians. But something much greater happened. Liz, an older woman in the group, asked Susan if she wanted to spend one-on-one time together for extra encouragement and accountability.

Of course, Susan was thrilled. Liz was such a spiritual giant in Susan's eyes! Susan expected that she would listen as Liz taught her all she needed to know about living a victorious Christian life. Not only did Liz know God's Word, but she also was the most compassionate woman Susan had ever met!

Susan's first surprise was that Liz was so low-key when they met together. She didn't lecture Susan or act super-spiritual. It was soon apparent that Liz really loved her, as a mother loves her daughter. Bit by bit, Susan opened up her heart to Liz, who was easy to talk to because she was transparent in sharing about her own struggles in her marriage, job and family. She taught Susan how to rely on Scripture for answers and prayed with her about everything.

Liz generously and selflessly poured out her life and Susan blossomed spiritually. A new Christian was brought to maturity because she had a Christlike role model. It happened easily and naturally as she experienced the love and patience of a spiritual parent. Now Susan has taken the step to become a spiritual parent herself, as she has learned through Liz's modeling.

Just how do spiritual young men and women grow up to become spiritual fathers and mothers? There is only one way— to have children! You could memorize the entire book of Leviticus and repeat it backward while standing on your head, but your knowledge and expertise would not make you a spiritual mentor. Spiritual parents become parents by having spiritual children. It is as simple as that!

You can become a spiritual parent either by adoption (parenting someone who is already a believer but who needs mentoring) or by natural birth (parenting someone you have personally led to Christ). Onesimus was a natural spiritual son to Paul while Timothy was a spiritual son by adoption. Paul led Onesimus to Christ while in prison (see Philem. 10). Paul met Timothy while in Lystra after Timothy had come to Christ earlier under the influence of his mother and grand-mother (see Acts 16:1-3). Paul treated both adopted son Timothy and natural son Onesimus as his spiritual sons and was committed to helping them mature spiritually. He called them both his sons.

Spiritual parents are mature believers who have grown and matured in their Christian walk and are ready to invest in the growth and maturity of others. They are called *fathers* according to 1 John 2:13: "I write to you, fathers, because you have known Him who is from the beginning . . ." This implies a profound and thorough knowledge of Jesus through His Word. It also implies a deep sense of passionate acquaintance with Him through His Holy Spirit. Mature Christians are awake to their calling to be like Jesus—to be a father in the way of God's Son. They understand what it takes to be a spiritual parent and are willing to become one.

I will never forget the experience of becoming a father for the first time. I faithfully attended prenatal classes where I learned how to coach LaVerne through her labor. After only three sessions, the nurse told us she would see us at the hospital. Scary.

When the contractions started, reality hit me and I hit the panic button. We were going to have a baby! (Well, okay, LaVerne was going to have a baby—but I was on the team.) I wasn't ready! I was too young. I was too inexperienced. I wanted to tell LaVerne,

"Couldn't you just put it on hold for a few months until we are ready for this?" But that was not an option. It was time, and LaVerne gave birth to a beautiful baby girl. And somehow, by the grace of God, we learned that we were more ready than we realized to be parents. Our own parents and friends were available for advice, and—amazingly enough—the baby did not break.

It is not easy to raise children, and most new parents feel unprepared when the first one comes along. Primed by racks of bestselling child-care manuals and how-to videos, parents are still uneasy about their ability to care for their child.

Just as many natural parents are unsure of their parenting skills, many potential spiritual parents feel insecure and uncertain. They simply do not feel ready! Yet one of the greatest catalysts for maturity as a Christian is becoming a spiritual mentor. Parenthood challenges and even changes our perspectives. We overcome spiritual pride and are stretched in all directions of growth. This is how the Lord planned it so that we can grow in maturity in Christ. Even if prospective spiritual parents do not feel ready, as they take a step of faith and draw on the help and advice of their own spiritual moms and dads, they will find great success and fulfillment and discover that they are more ready than they realized.

Yasuko came as a Japanese exchange student to attend a university near Harrisburg, Pennsylvania. Her host family, who served in a small group in our church, accepted her as one of the family and included her in all family activities, including a small-group Bible study that met in their community. Although her Buddhist parents had warned her to remain true to her upbringing, Yasuko was overwhelmed by the love and acceptance showered on her by these Christians.

Just two days before Christmas, her host family found her crying. When asked the reason for her tears, Yasuko explained, "I am so happy! I am going to give you a Christmas gift. I want to tell you that today I gave my life to Jesus!" Her host family and small group rejoiced! For the remaining few months that Yasuko had in America, they became spiritual parents to her and helped her mature from a spiritual newborn to a spiritual young adult.

Yasuko returned to Japan and became a spiritual mother to many others as she continued to receive spiritual parenting via email from her spiritual mom and dad in Pennsylvania. She served as a youth leader in Japan and eventually went on to become a missionary to China, all while continuing to be mentored by her spiritual parents in America.

When parenting those who are spiritually parenting others, mentors should:

• Give their spiritual protégés many opportunities to minister and to serve others.

• Give honest, loving constructive input to help them grow spiritually.

• Try to work themselves out of a job. Whatever role they presently have, mentors should ask the Lord if He is calling their spiritual son or daughter to take their place so that they can move on to something new the Lord may have for them.

• Open doors for their spiritual sons or daughters that will enhance their ministry as spiritual parents to others.

• Ask them, "If you were me, what would you do differently?" and "What would you like to be doing 5 or 10 years down the road?" Then help them get there.

Although a spiritual parent should be mature enough to give freely without thought of return, I think it is a good idea for a son or daughter to look for ways to bless his or her spiritual mentor. Parents need encouragement, too! Occasionally they need to hear the actual words that they are having an impact on the lives of those they are mentoring. Words and actions of blessing are powerful. Spiritual children can bless their parents by sending cards of appreciation, giving spontaneous gifts or telling them by communicating words of encouragement face to face.

I firmly believe the following biblical promise to natural children also applies to spiritual children: "Honor your father and mother, which is the first commandment with promise: that it may be well with you and you may live long on the earth" (Eph. 6:2-3).

As mentors encourage their spiritual children to grow up and have their own spiritual children, the relationship changes. Now spiritual parents talk to their son or daughter about their own parenting experiences. Spiritual mentors continue to parent their grown-up spiritual children as long as they need the input, but in some ways, the children eventually become peers. When children are babies, their parents meet all of their needs. When parents are elderly, the children often assume a role of responsibility for the well-being of the parents. Be aware of the possibilities of these potential changes in spiritual parenting relationships.

YOU *CAN* REACH PARENTHOOD!

I was captivated by author Henri J. M. Nouwen's description of his journey to spiritual fatherhood in his book *The Return of the Prodigal Son.* In it, he tells of his fascination with Rembrandt's painting of the prodigal son in his father's arms with the elder son looking on.

"Am I the elder son or the prodigal in that picture?" Nouwen agonized over the years as he searched for spiritual fulfillment. One day, a friend looked at him and spoke these powerful words:

> Whether you are the younger son or the elder son, you have to realize that you are called to become the father. You have been looking for friends all your life; you have been craving for affection as long as I've known you; you have been interested in thousands of things; you have been begging for attention, appreciation, and affirmation left and right. The time has come to claim your true vocation—to be a father who can welcome his children home without asking them any questions and without wanting anything from them in return.[2]

Like the father of the prodigal son, a spiritual father gives himself joyfully to his son because he loves him. Equipped with this affirmation and love, a son can claim his sonship, to grow up and become a healthy father himself. Becoming mature requires selflessness, as Nouwen's friend pointed out. A selfless person gives people the opportunity to come through or fail while still loving them.

Whatever stage you are at in your spiritual growth and maturity, God's call on your life is eventually to become a mature spiritual parent, loving His children as He loves them—selflessly and without condition.

PART II

FINDING A SPIRITUAL MENTOR

CHAPTER 5

LOOKING FOR A
SPIRITUAL PARENT

 Key: If you do not have a spiritual
mentor, begin by becoming one.

There are three vital spiritual relationships that every healthy, growing person needs. The most common of these are what I call "Barnabas relationships." These are the connections we have with our peers. Barnabas was the kind of person who saw beyond people's pasts and weaknesses and believed in their potential. He came alongside the new convert Paul and convinced the skeptical believers in Jerusalem that Paul was indeed a Christian and would no longer persecute them. While this connection began as a mentoring relationship, it later grew into a peer relationship as Paul and Barnabas became traveling companions on a missionary journey. The Antioch church set Paul and Barnabas apart and sent them off as part of a team. They were peers who worked together.

Just like Paul and Barnabas, we all need peers in our lives. Teenagers should have peer relationships with teenagers, parents with parents, doctors with doctors, pastors with pastors, and so forth.

The second relationship we need as spiritually maturing people is a "Paul relationship." Spiritual sons and daughters have this kind of connection with their spiritual mentors. Paul regularly referred to Timothy as his child or son[1] and also referred to others of his converts in this way.[2] None of these young men were Paul's biological sons, but they related to him as their spiritual father.

Third, there are "Timothy relationships." These are the connections spiritual parents have with the spiritual sons and daughters whom they mentor, as we have explored.

It may seem ideal to begin with Barnabas and Paul relationships and then move on to Timothy-type mentoring, but we cannot always build these connections in one particular order. Sometimes we must start where we are.

Peter and John had no formal education, but they spoke fluently to the scholarly religious leaders of the Sanhedrin: "When they saw the courage of Peter and John and realized that they were unschooled, ordinary men, they were astonished and they took note that these men *had been with Jesus*" (Acts 4:13, emphasis added).

A spiritual father does not have to be a spiritual giant in order to train others. No one is a finished product. We are all learning to live in obedience to God and growing in grace. What really counts is our hearts and Who resides there. The important thing is that we "have been with Jesus."

God takes common, ordinary people who love Jesus and transforms them by His presence. Spiritual growth is recognizing who God calls us to be and overcoming obstacles that stand in the way of maturity through the power of the Holy Spirit. God can use us to mentor others at any point in our Christian walk if we allow Him free rein in our lives.

As a young man, I worked on a construction crew building new houses. I learned that the first step to building a sturdy house is to put in a solid concrete foundation. It takes time to level the blocks and secure them with concrete, but a solid foundation keeps the house safe when the inevitable storms and wind come. This same principle is true of our spiritual lives. To become spiritual parents, we begin by building a firm foundation on Jesus Christ. We get to know Jesus intimately and surrender all that we are and hope to be to Him. Only then can we be the safe and secure refuge He calls us to be for others.

WHEN IS THE TIME RIGHT?

Perhaps you are one of the many believers who have never had a spiritual mentor, a Paul relationship; this does not mean that you are unable to be one. If you feel you cannot become a spiritual parent until you have been mentored yourself, break out of that small mindset! Instead, take a step of faith and see what the Lord will do. God's Word says we will reap what we sow (see Gal. 6:7). Sow whatever God has given you into another's life and God will likely bring a spiritual parent into your life.

If you wait until you think you are ready to begin a Timothy connection with a younger believer, it will probably never happen. You don't need to be perfect, just faithful and obedient. Mother Teresa once said, "God does not demand that I be successful. God demands that I be faithful. When facing God, results are not important. Faithfulness is what is important."[3]

God knows both when we need a spiritual parent and when we are ready to become one. Abraham looked expectantly for a city designed and built by God, but lived in a tent like a wanderer because the timing for God's promise was not yet right. Moses missed the timing of God when he killed an Egyptian, but God gave him another chance. The timing was finally right 40 years later when the Lord called Moses at the burning bush to lead his people out of bondage. Jesus worked in His earthly father's carpentry shop until the time appointed by the heavenly Father for Him to begin His public ministry. Later, Jesus infuriated the religious leaders of His day by His claims of deity, and they wanted to kill Him immediately. But "his *time had not yet come*" (John 7:30, emphasis added) and Jesus continued to preach until the time appointed by the Father came for Him to go to Calvary (see John 13:1). God has the right time and the right relationships planned for us; we need only to seek His direction and obey.

WHERE DO I BEGIN?

Whether you are a potential spiritual mentor or hopeful protégé, the first place to begin a relationship is in prayer. Start by praying that God will reveal the person you should mentor or who might potentially mentor you. If you have tried in the past and it has not worked out, continue to pray and trust Him for His divine connections.

One of the most difficult aspects of a mentoring relationship is finding the right person. Many times, the best relationships happen "naturally": A conversation begins, then a few more conversations, and soon you realize you have a mentor or protégé. But there is no magic formula for initiating a relationship. You just have to go and do it. Every person is unique and will find what works for them. Although it is more common for the mentor to initiate the relationship—this is the way Jesus approached His disciples—the initiation of a relationship can go either way. The mentor may ask the protégé, or vice versa.

There should be a mutual attraction that draws the mentor and protégé together. If it is God's will, He will take that initial attraction and pull the relationship together in His timing. Your job in either role is to be the kind of person who is open, approachable and willing. Develop a reputation as a person who listens lovingly and attentively to others, and you will be surprised how "naturally" connections occur.

One approach to initiating a relationship is to identify commonalities you share with a potential mentor or protégé, such as church, children, sports or similar spiritual gifts. This person may be a friend, a co-worker, a relative, in a small group you attend, in your local church or a person involved in ministry with you. Look for someone you feel comfortable working with and who will probably feel comfortable working with you, and then dare to make the first move!

Or perhaps you see someone who needs encouragement. Initiate a relationship by helping in practical ways. Babysit for a single mom so that she can have a night out. Go to the grocery store for a mother with toddlers. Spend time with a single person who seems lonely. Invite a younger person into your home to watch a ball game or for tea, and write notes or make encouraging phone calls to that individual. Get to know his or her history. Share your testimonies with each other. Study a book together. Spend time together in Bible study if he or she is a young Christian and needs to be grounded in the Word. Discover their areas of struggle and pray for them. If you are already a friend, you may feel God's tug at your heart to open your life more fully and transparently. Take a risk and be vulnerable. Make the time to invest in the relationship and be strong on encouragement. As the relationship unfolds, you will experience the closeness of true spiritual friendship.

How Do I Know I'm on the Right Track?

The relationship, of course, must be *mutual*, because the purpose of any mentoring relationship is mutual spiritual improvement and benefit. A key to successful mentoring is that both the mentor and protégé desire to receive guidance and help. There must be a sense on both sides that there is reciprocal investment in the relationship. Both the spiritual parent and the son or daughter must recognize their need for the relationship. "Can two walk together, unless they are agreed?" (Amos 3:3). When there is mutual faith for the relationship, we are assured of its healthy existence, because faith is God-ordained (see Eph. 2:8).

Both must want the relationship to work so that everyone can improve personally and spiritually, but the spiritual mentor should seek to understand what his son or daughter desires to gain from the relationship. Then, with those expectations clearly understood, the spiritual parent aims to fulfill their son or daughter's hopes by tapping into their own observations and experiences.

It is also essential for the spiritual parent and their son or daughter to enjoy and *like* being with one another. I like how Gunter Krallman describes how and why Jesus recruited His followers:

> As a leader Jesus knew that the success or failure of his mission would decisively depend on the selection of the right helpers. Thus he took the initiative in calling men to become disciples, a step as unprecedented in rabbinic tradition as the fact that he called them to follow not just his teaching but him as a person. Jesus did not merely recruit them for their intellectual benefit or for a task, he recruited them for a relationship.[4]

In other words, in addition to training them, Jesus wanted *fellowship* with them. He loved them and enjoyed spending time with each one. He called the Twelve that they might *be with Him* (see Mark 3:14). Love is the pivotal point on which a spiritual mentoring relationship rests.

I find it interesting to note that though the word "disciple" is used 225 times in the Gospels, Jesus Himself only used it two

times. Jesus preferred instead to use the word "friend." More
than wanting disciples or apprentices to train, Jesus wanted to
be in a loving friendship with the spiritual sons He was mentoring. He knew that anyone can impress people from a distance,
but you can only affect lives for eternity when you're up close
and personal.

What If I've Tried and Failed?

A few years ago, Murray McCall, who has spent 10 years in
church planting in New Zealand, told me, "After going through
a season of discouragement as a spiritual leader, I came to understand that God had called me to be a father." This truth set
him free as a leader in the Body of Christ. He realized that his
primary call was to be a father, and he could trust God for grace
to start again when he made mistakes or was discouraged.

The Bible is filled with examples and models for us to imitate: the impartation from Moses to Joshua, from Elijah to
Elisha, from Samuel to David, from Paul to Timothy and Titus.
Regardless of disappointments or mistakes made along the
way, every Christian must seek godly courage to become a
spiritual father or mother and impart to others what God has
given to them. It is possible and achievable, no matter what is
in the past!

Dan Hitzhusen is a church planter who fondly recalls how
his spiritual father, Josh McDowell, responded to his mistakes
as a young leader:

Josh saw me as a diamond in the rough. I was twenty-one
years old with a heart for God, full of life, and full of
myself. Serving as a personal assistant to Josh McDowell
as a staff member of Campus Crusade for Christ, I made
many mistakes. Josh expected excellence, yet, when I blew

it, he would say something like, "Dan, that just shows it can happen to the best of them."

I remember really messing something up and asking Josh why he didn't get particularly angry with me. He said, "Dan, the things that I think will make you a better person, a better friend, a better representative of Jesus Christ, I share with you. Everything else I take to God."

On another occasion, I was feeling rejected by some of my co-workers. Josh pulled me aside and said, "Dan, you and I are renegades. We are different. We will never really fit in. You will never fit in. That isn't the way God made you."

Josh always believed in me more than I believed in myself.

Perhaps the greatest personal tribute that I have for Josh McDowell is that he saw me for who God made me to be and he encouraged me to serve God with my whole heart in my own uniqueness.[5]

Though Dan experienced disillusionment with himself and with others, his mentor never doubted that God had great plans for his life. No matter what you have experienced or perpetrated in the past, God has plans for your life, too.

The Lord is placing a desire within mature Christians of our generation to be spiritual fathers and mothers to the next generation. Relationships between the young and the old are a key to the Kingdom. The Lord wants to bring the young and the old together, bind them close to each other and to their God, and teach them to build His kingdom together. All it takes is willingness, availability, time and a generous dose of the grace of God. Open your hands and heart and look to Him for grace and direction. He will mend and redeem everything that is past for His glory.

Wait No Longer!

After having experienced the lack of a spiritual father in my life for about 10 years, I made the decision to become a spiritual father to others. Amazingly enough, as I reached out to others who needed guidance and security and became a spiritual father to them, the Lord brought spiritual fathers into my own life.

I want to emphasize this: *Don't wait until you find a spiritual father or mother—become one yourself!* Waiting to acquire that wonderful spiritual mentor who will perfectly nurture and love you before you reach out to parent others is like saying of your natural childhood, "My childhood was terrible. I grew up in a dysfunctional family. I'll never have kids because I would be a terrible parent." This is simply not true! Each parent can begin with a clean slate. Parents, both natural and spiritual, can decide to learn from the past and make good choices along the way. If we wait until we receive all the spiritual nurturing we feel we need before we reach out to others, we will never fulfill the plan God has for each of us: growing into spiritual parenthood.

The Scriptures tell us to "cast your bread upon the waters, for you will find it after many days" (Eccles. 11:1). Reaching out to parent another may look to you like throwing away your chance for having your own needs met, but when you sow into others' lives, God promises that you will reap a return.

I was teaching on spiritual fathering and mothering at a pastor's conference in Portland, Oregon, and an elderly man approached me between sessions. "I have been a spiritual father for many years," he began. "I was a staff member for Campus Crusade for Christ, and I was a spiritual father to students in the university. But I never had a spiritual father myself. Recently, however, I moved to Florida and began to attend a new church. A young man in church leadership approached me and asked me to go out for breakfast. After we ordered, he asked how I was doing and if I had any areas in my life that needed prayer. He wanted to pray for me on a regular basis. After our breakfast was over, he asked me to meet him again. And our breakfasts have continued since." Then the elderly man looked at me with a twinkle in his eye. "Larry, I now have a spiritual father. He is 29 years old!"

Allow God to put together spiritual mentoring relationships in His time. Become the spiritual father or mother He has called you to be and watch how He is able to bring exactly what you need. When you "cast your bread upon the waters," expect it to return!

Chapter 6

Security in the Father's Love

 Key: Only God can meet your need for a father's love.

Millions of people today believe that God is the Creator of the universe, but far fewer choose to know Him deeply enough to experience Him as their Father. Yet in His intercessory prayer, Jesus claimed that it is possible to know God in this way: "Now this is eternal life: that they may know you, the only true God, and Jesus Christ, whom you have sent" (John 17:3). God revealed Himself to us through Jesus Christ, and the entire gospel rests on this claim: that knowing God, through Jesus, brings abundant, eternal life. Our Father is a God of relationship. He wants to be our Father and have a personal friendship with us, and through that relationship to reveal His ways to us. When we know the Father and develop a love relationship with Him, we are secure as believers, willing and ready to reach out to others in love.

No earthly friendship, including the very best of mentoring relationships, can substitute for this connection with the Father. Only the love of the Lord can impact our lives deeply enough to create lasting change, to transform our lives for eternity. Whether you are a mentor or a protégé, it is imperative that you keep your relationship with the Father primary, over and above all others. As your friendship with God deepens, you will become increasingly freed and equipped to relate to others as a spiritual parent or a spiritual son or daughter, secure and grounded in the foundation of the Father's love.

SECURE TO GIVE LOVE FREELY

Jesus knew He was a love gift from the Father to the world. He knew where He came from. He knew why He was here and where He was going. Because of this confidence, Jesus was secure in His calling and mission: to freely and lovingly give of Himself without hesitation. As He mentored His disciples and passed on the love that came from the Father, they in turn learned to give love freely without holding back.

If we are to grow into healthy spiritual fathers and mothers, we must be confident of our Father's love for us and live in close relationship with Him. Only secure spiritual parents, who are totally convinced that the heavenly Father loves them, can freely and lovingly pass on a healthy spiritual inheritance to the next generation.

And only sons and daughters who are grounded in their heavenly Father's love can freely receive, take in and pass on the grace and wisdom they gain from their spiritual mentors. Why do you think Jesus' disciples turned the world upside down in a few short years? They didn't change the world because they attended all the right seminars, but because they lived in close, intimate relationship with the right Person and couldn't wait to freely pass on the overflowing abundance of God's love!

John, one of the 12 disciples of Jesus, became a father to the next generation of believers as he grew secure in the love of his heavenly Father. The Bible shows us that John and Jesus enjoyed an intimate, special friendship. When writing his Gospel, John identified himself repeatedly as "the disciple whom Jesus loved." He recorded that at the Passover supper, as was customary of the Greeks and Romans at mealtime, he reclined beside the Master, "leaning on Jesus' bosom" (John 13:23), an indication of close friendship and affection. While standing near the cross during Jesus' crucifixion, he referred to himself as the "one whom Jesus loved" (John 19:26) and did so again in his account of the resurrection (see John 20:2). He called himself "the disciple whom Jesus loved" when he told Peter "It is the Lord!" after Jesus was raised from the dead (see John 21:7). When Jesus exhorted Peter regarding how he would die, Peter asked, "What about him?" (referring to John) and again John named himself "the disciple Jesus loved" (John 21:20-23).

I think it's clear that John was totally convinced he was accepted and loved by Jesus! He knew Jesus like a brother and was a devoted friend. He was secure in the love of his Master. But how did John come to such a state of confidence and security in his life, enabling him to mentor and serve countless later followers of Jesus? It did not happen overnight.

Before he matured under the mentoring guidance of Jesus' loving influence, John's actions and attitudes were, to understate the matter, less than secure. He was hungry for status and power and seems to have had quite a few rough edges. John and his brother James were nicknamed the "sons of thunder" (Mark 3:17). I picture them as tough guys, perhaps the equivalent of modern inner-city gangsters, who secretly longed for security, belonging and identity. The brothers evidently had fiery tempers. When some Samaritans refused to allow Jesus and His disciples to come through their village, James and John asked Jesus if they could order fire down from heaven to burn up the inhospitable town (see Luke 9:54). At that point in John's life, he certainly was not modeling the loving, giving Spirit of Christ!

John and his brother earned the anger of the other disciples when they asked if they could sit on Jesus' right and left hand in glory (see Mark 10:35-45). In one case, they even sent their mother to implore Jesus for special favors, showing tell-tale signs of insecurity and self-seeking (see Matt. 20:20-21). And yet another time, John saw a man driving out demons in Jesus' name, a man who was not a part of the "in group." In John's immaturity he tried to stop the exorciser, and Jesus rebuked him for his insecure, sectarian attitude that caused him to exclude others who sought to follow Him (see Luke 9:49-50).

Later, however, we see that John imparted the Holy Spirit to Philip's converts in Samaria, the very people on whom he had wanted to call down fire for refusing to hear the gospel (see Acts 8:14-16). It's obvious that something occurred in John's life in the intervening years. What happened was this: As John spent more time with Jesus, he was changed. Lengthy exposure to Jesus' extravagant love tranformed the "son of thunder" into "the disciple whom Jesus loved."

In his Gospel, John recorded that Jesus told His disciples the secret of His love for them: "As the Father has loved me, so I have loved you" (John 15:9). How amazing! John received a revelation from Jesus that his Lord loved him just as much and in the same way as the Father loved His Son. This revelation opened the doors of John's heart so that he could give love freely to the next generation.

Even more amazing is that we are loved by the Father in the same way. When we become confident and secure in this knowledge, the doors of our hearts are opened to love freely and without hesitation. It is not enough to experience God's perfect love—we must also be willing to give that love away, just as God did: "God so loved the world that He *gave* . . ." (John 3:16, emphasis added). Giving love away helps us to live up to our full potential in God. It releases the joy of the Lord in our lives!

How do we give love away? By modeling God's love as we point our spiritual children to Jesus. In this way, love is multiplied through them. When our spiritual children see that we know the Father, they will want that same intimate, loving relationship for themselves. They see, by our vibrant prayer life and friendship with the Lord, that we are in love with Jesus. They will want to experience firsthand the blessed knowledge that their heavenly Father loves them.

But spiritual children must be careful that they do not rely on their mentor's love more than they rely on the love of Jesus. Remember: Nothing can replace the heavenly Father's love in our lives. Years ago, before I ever heard of the term "spiritual fathering," I mentored some young men who wanted to grow in their new Christian lives. In my zeal, unfortunately, I provided too much security for them, rather than allowing them to discover how to place their total trust in Jesus. They began looking to me for that which only our Father in heaven could give them. Our mentoring relationship became an unhealthy bondage.

Looking to any leader for all the answers and putting him or her up on a spiritual pedestal is dangerous, because they are likely to fall off at one point or another! No wonder those I mentored become disillusioned and wounded; I did not have all the answers and I made mistakes, and because they were not grounded in the Father's love, my failures hurt them more than was necessary.

I learned a valuable lesson about the delicate balance of pointing people to the Father while mentoring them to grow spiritually. We can mentor and be mentored effectively only if we rely completely on God's grace. Spiritual parents must constantly direct their protégé's gaze toward Jesus, and spiritual children must strive to focus on their relationship with the heavenly Father before any other. We can never have our emotional and spiritual needs met by the love of a spiritual mentor. We must know our heavenly Father and experience His love and unconditional acceptance.

Charles Spurgeon once said, "The sheep are never so safe from the wolf as when they are near the shepherd." A close personal relationship with Jesus will keep spiritual children safe from harm because their foundation, grounded in the Father's love, will be strong. And out of that security and confidence, they will, in turn, give love freely.

SECURE TO SERVE OTHERS

In the upper room during His last supper with His disciples, Jesus was so completely secure in the Father's love that He was able to serve His spiritual sons and expect nothing in return. The Gospel of John states:

> Jesus knew that the Father had put all things under his power, and that he had come from God and was returning to God; so he got up from the meal, took off his outer clothing, and wrapped a towel around his waist. After that, he poured water into a basin and began to wash his disciples' feet, drying them with the towel that was wrapped around him (13:3-5).

Mark, the author of the Gospel of Mark, was a spiritual son of the apostle Peter (see 1 Pet. 5:13) who probably didn't have the privilege of witnessing Jesus' sacrificial service to His disciples in the upper room. Whether or not his shortcomings were due to not seeing Jesus firsthand, the evidence suggests that Mark had some problems accepting the heavenly Father's love. I believe it was this lack of solid grounding and confidence that resulted in a few problems when he was called on to serve. He deserted Paul on the apostle's first mission trip, and at the start of another missionary journey Paul refused to allow Mark to accompany him. This caused a rift between Barnabas and Paul, with Paul rejecting Mark and Barnabas choosing to take the young man with him (see Acts 15:38-40).

Imagine being the unfortunate person responsible for splitting up the greatest church-planting team in history! In spite of Mark's shaky beginnings, however, Paul later forgave his wavering ways, telling the Colossian church to welcome him (see Col. 4:10) and then asking Mark to come and help him in his continuing ministry (see 2 Tim. 4:11).

I believe that somewhere along the way, Mark had a profound experience of his heavenly Father's love in addition to the persistent love of his spiritual fathers, Barnabas and Peter. It also must have helped that he had a praying mother; her house was a home to many praying people, including Peter (see Acts 12:12). Mark changed from a deserter to a faithful and useful servant of Christ because he received a revelation that Jesus loved him unconditionally. The combination of a growing intimacy with the Father and the nurturing influence of spiritual parents on Mark's life caused him to grow up spiritually, ready to serve out of his grounding and confidence in God's love.

When we become intimate with our heavenly Father and are willing to be influenced by faithful mentors, we too will be molded into the kind of people useful for service in God's kingdom. Knowing the Father transforms us and matures us into spiritual adulthood. Experiencing the reality of His love causes us to grow from spiritual babies to spiritual young men and women, and encourages us to take the next step to becoming spiritual parents.

The apostle John also learned how to serve humbly, following the example set by his Master. When Jesus asked him to prepare the Passover supper, he did so willingly (see Luke 22:8), and from this we can see the transformation love had already worked in his life. He no longer asked for special favors, but instead was willing to serve. John had learned, by spending time with Jesus, that love knows no bounds and should be extended even to those initially antagonistic to the gospel, such as the Samaritans. Getting to know Jesus intimately caused John to love as Jesus loved—fully and unconditionally, in service born from love.

John wrote the First, Second and Third Epistles of John, which are sometimes called the "books of love" because they are written from the heart of a loving father to his spiritual children. By that time, John was thoroughly secure in his Father's love and longed to nurture and serve the scattered Church. Even later in life when John was exiled to the Isle of Patmos, where he wrote the book of Revelation, he continued to serve the growing Body of Christ from afar, confident and grounded in God's love for him. Jesus' love molded John into a revered and loved disciple who spent his life in service to the Father and His children.

Like John, we must be willing to serve the Lord in any way He asks. And when we know God loves us completely and unconditionally, we will be willing to do whatever He directs and serve wherever He sends us.

Secure Whether or Not Others Affirm Us

During the early 1990s, I went through a season when I felt like a failure in ministry and leadership. Though I was serving as the pastor of a rapidly growing church, I wanted to quit. Even with all of the outward signs of success, I was tired and felt unappreciated and misunderstood. I secretly thought it would be better to leave church leadership behind and go back into the business world.

In the midst of my struggle, I stopped in to see Steve Prokopchak, our staff counselor. I asked him for his evaluation of the reasons I was not able to lead in a way that some on our team felt was appropriate and effective. Steve gently offered me some kind advice, and then encouraged me to listen to a cassette tape he thought might be helpful.

In the car a few days later, I popped the cassette into my tape player to see what the speaker had to say. He immediately caught my attention as he talked about leaders who have a "messiah complex," who feel that they need to have all the answers and be everyone's savior. I was glued to the speaker's words, and it almost seemed as if he was talking directly to my situation.

Then it dawned on me: *I* was the speaker on the tape! I rarely listen to recordings of myself and had not recognized my own voice. Then it all came back to me—I had taught a pastors' training course at our church the year before, and the recording captured my words to the future pastors, encouraging them to recognize the Lord as the only one who could ultimately meet their needs. A year later, I had not taken my own medicine, and I was paying for it!

On Steve's advice and with the affirmation of the leadership team of our church, I took a three-month sabbatical. It took me about five weeks just to feel human again; but during those months off, I began to deeply understand that significance and security cannot come from what I do or from what people think of me. In an undeniable and personal way, the Lord revealed that my value comes from His love for me. And God loves me just because He loves me, not because of what I do or what people think.

I keenly remember pacing back and forth in a cabin in the mountains, reading aloud from the Scriptures over and over again: "I have chosen you and have not rejected you. So do not fear, for I am with you; do not be dismayed, for I am your God . . . For I am the Lord, your God, who takes hold of your right hand and says to you, 'Do not fear; I will help you'" (Isa. 41:9-10,13). During a time of disillusionment and near burn-out, I finally accepted that my significance comes from God's love for me, and that alone.

Although I had known this to be theologically correct for years, it had never sunk deeply into my spirit. The song I had learned as a child, "Jesus loves me, this I know, for the Bible tells me so," took on fresh meaning. I was changed! Whether or not people liked me or affirmed me was no longer an issue (of course it is still nice when they do), because I knew in my bones that God loves me!

I was now whole because I had personally experienced the Father's love in a real way. I did not need the affirmation of others, including my spiritual children; I had received the affirmation of my Father in heaven. Now I could be a spiritually and emotionally healthy spiritual father to others.

The transforming power of Jesus' love relationship with His disciple John demonstrates the singular importance of a close friendship with God. John loved and served his spiritual children without concerning himself with their affirmation or approval, grounded in a confidence that came from knowing he was safe and secure in the love of the Father. We can love and serve out of that same confidence, whether as mentors or spiritual children, and it starts with us deeply knowing that "Jesus loves me, this I know, for the Bible tells me so." So simple, yet so powerful!

CHAPTER 7

HEALING THE PAST

 Key: God can restore us to healthy mentoring relationships.

If a spiritual parent or their potential protégé has been wounded in the past in a mentoring relationship, it is incredibly important for both their sakes to seek healing. People with unhealed emotional and spiritual wounds have a strong tendency to inflict similar wounds on others.

Here we look at a few common ways people may have been hurt through mentoring relationships and how to seek healing for those wounds.

PAIN FROM UNHEALTHY MENTORING

Abuse of Authority

Abuse of power warps the blessing of spiritual fathering and mothering. Spiritual fathers and mothers are not to be dominating authority figures who coerce their children into submission. Instead, they are to tread lightly as they point their spiritual children to Jesus. I like how Floyd McClung describes the much-needed balance we need to exercise in the area of spiritual fathering and mothering in his book *The Father Heart of God*:

Godly fathers want to serve others, and treat all men and women as their equals. Their actions proceed from an attitude of equality, not authority, because they are more concerned with serving than ruling. Biblical authority is never taken; it is offered. . . . It comes from the anointing of God's Spirit and is the sum total of one's character, wisdom, spiritual gift, and servant attitude. Fathers in the Lord understand these principles about authority. They know the character of the Father, so they are relaxed in their ministry to other people . . . they have learned to take action as God directs, and not just because they are "the leader."[1]

Healthy spiritual fathers earn the right to speak into their sons' lives because they do so with the heart of a servant, affirming and encouraging them in their walk with Christ. A level of trust is built over time in a balanced relationship that encourages sons and daughters to be dependent on God.

If you are a spiritual parent or a spiritual child who is in a mentoring relationship that is abusive, seek outside help now. Unhealthy relational ties can be very hard to discern when you are so close, and even harder to disengage. Seek the counsel of your pastor or another church leader who is somewhat removed from the relationship. Be honest about what is taking place, allow them to evaluate the dynamics of the relationship and follow their guidance for restoring or bringing the relationship to a close. Above all, cover the situation in prayer.

Or perhaps you feel hindered in the present by some of the experiences you had in the past. Maybe you were abused, hurt, disappointed, held back or lacked a healthy role model to follow. The Lord has a great plan for you. You can be restored!

The enemies of God's people ridiculed Nehemiah and his workers as they started to rebuild the wall around Jerusalem.

The wall had been broken down for ages and the stones were charred and useless. How did these people think they could do anything with the mess? "Can these burned stones live?" they mocked (see Neh. 4:2). They did not want to see Jerusalem become secure and safe again, because they wanted to continue running roughshod over its boundaries.

The devil is throwing similar accusations at God's people today: "How does that Christian think he can function with all the baggage from that broken relationship with his father?" or "You've made too many mistakes, how do you expect to help someone else?" Perhaps we sincerely tried reaching out to another and the relationship deteriorated, so we feel like a failure. Maybe a spiritual father we looked up to used control and legalism to get his point across. Devastated and hurt, we tell ourselves we will never place ourselves in a position to be hurt again. These damaging thoughts come from the devil, who wants to rob us of hope and can keep us defeated and discouraged.

We must believe that although our own resources are few, we can be restored to carry out God's work. We can place our full trust in the overruling providence of God. The burned stones of Jerusalem's wall were charred and looked useless, but God's people chose not to look at the dismal circumstances. Instead, they trusted the Lord. Because they refused to listen to their enemies' discouraging words, they succeeded in rebuilding the wall.

Abandonment

Have you ever felt that someone "dropped" you, crippling you for life? I meet so many people with a clear call of God on their lives who feel they have been burned emotionally or abandoned by someone they trusted. Some were burned by the deterioration of a relationship they had invested in and developed.

In other cases, they were disillusioned when a natural father or a spiritual father disappointed them, and they gave up. These wounded people often live in deep disappointment and fear that they will never be loved and that the Lord will never be able to use them.

Not too many years ago, Cedric, who now leads a thriving church in East Africa, felt burned. He had worked side by side with a missionary and planted nearly 400 churches in his native country. He looked to this man as a spiritual father, but the relationship began to unravel when Cedric started to notice that money was the bottom line for the missionary. The missionary cared little about the souls brought to the Lord through church planting; he was motivated by financial gain. He didn't love his spiritual son as Cedric believed—he was using Cedric to enrich himself.

Cedric attempted to untangle himself from the missionary's web of deception and greed, narrowly escaping harm when the missionary sent thugs to burn Cedric's house down. Shell-shocked and grieved, and reluctant to ever trust again, Cedric moved to a neighboring nation and enrolled in a university. While there, he fellowshipped at a church where people reached out in love to him. As he was restored, he took a step of faith to take up his mantle as a spiritual father. God began to use him as a leader in small-group ministry, and he later returned to his native country to plant a church.

Cedric was willing to start over because he refused to be intimidated by Satan's discouraging lies. This burned stone was healed! Today, he serves as a spiritual father to pastors all over his nation.

If Cedric's wounded heart and spirit can be restored, yours can be, too. Let's explore the ways God brings healing through faith to those who have been abused, abandoned, burned and wounded.

Restoration to Healthy Mentoring

Believe the Past Can Be Redeemed

In the first chapter of Matthew, we read the genealogy of Jesus. Why was this very long list of "begats" included in God's Word? Two reasons are that it demonstrates how people, specifically families, are important to God, and it shows how a family can thrive and be blessed in the midst of the successes and failures of its individual members.

God wants families to pass on a blessing to the next generation. The Bible is a book recorded for the generations as a record of the rich inheritance of relationships down through the generations. God honors and places importance on a family's lineage because each family has a unique story to tell. The people included in Jesus' genealogy had a part in seeing Jesus trained and fathered during His years on earth. God the Father put Jesus on loan to Joseph and Mary so that they could train Him. Jesus' "foster father" trained Him in a carpentry shop. In order for Joseph to train Jesus, there had to be faithful individuals in his lineage who passed on a legacy of training. The life of Jesus was based on previous generations whose faithfulness had a direct bearing on His ministry.

In the same way, if we are to pass on an inheritance to others, we must receive a spiritual blessing from generations past. We need healthy spiritual fathers and mothers to deposit a rich inheritance into spiritual sons and daughters.

Sometimes, however, previous generations feel more like skeletons in the closet than legacies of inheritance. Jesus' genealogy includes Rahab, a prostitute who delivered the wicked city of Jericho to the Israelites. But the Lord redeemed Rahab's sinful past and what was passed down through the generations was her obedience to God and compassion for the Israelites—not her shame. Her salvation is evidence that God redeems and restores future generations when even one individual turns to God in faith. Even an ungodly family member can be redeemed and the entire next generation turned to the Lord.

We must build on the shoulders of those who have gone before us, regardless of the mistakes they have made. We need to live in a posture of praise to the Lord for those who birthed us and nourished us both naturally and spiritually, and expect Him to redeem any shame in generations past. And we must purpose in our hearts that, by the grace of God, we will be a positive influence on and give a good inheritance to the next generation.

Believe God, Not the Lies of the Enemy

We cannot believe the lies of the enemy and expect to live victoriously. If we justify our current negative situation by blaming it on past bad experiences, we will wallow in bitterness and unforgiveness. If we feel unable to fulfill the Lord's call on our lives because we have believed the lies of the enemy, we will be spiritually paralyzed and unable to fulfill our mandate as spiritual parents.

Mephibosheth was a young man we read about in the Bible who lived the first part of his life believing a lie. He hid out in the town of Lo Debar, believing his life was in great danger. Because his grandfather Saul was no longer the king of Israel, he was told it was only a matter of time until David, the new king, found and killed him. He had been told the stories about the new king and that, for generations, when a new king came into power, all family members of the former king were decapitated.

Mephibosheth lived not only in emotional pain but physical pain as well. While still a small child, he was crippled when a servant girl dropped him as they were fleeing from the new king's advance on the palace. He was emotionally and physically scarred, and like the stones of the fallen wall around Jerusalem, he was burned and broken—unable to fulfill his destiny.

One dreaded day, the new king's servants arrived in Lo Debar to find the grandson of King Saul. When they brought him to the palace, Mephibosheth fell on his face in terror and prostrated himself before King David, awaiting the death sentence that he knew must be next. But then, Mephibosheth couldn't believe his ears when he heard the king say, "Do not fear, for I will surely show you kindness for Jonathan your father's sake, and will restore to you all the land of Saul your grandfather; and you shall eat bread at my table continually" (2 Sam. 9:7).

Unknown to Mephibosheth, David had made a covenant with Mephibosheth's father, Jonathan, years before. They had pledged to take care of each other's families if anything ever happened to them. When Jonathan was killed in battle with his father, Saul, David remembered his covenant with his best friend. And he was committed to keeping his promise!

For years, Mephibosheth had believed a lie. He was convinced that David would kill him, but all the while David was pursuing him with his best interests at heart. Mephibosheth was esteemed by David and given the honor of sitting at the king's table. Every need Mephibosheth had was completely met.

In the same way, our King longs to meet our needs for spiritual growth and deep relationship. If we believe the lies of the enemy instead of believing that He will guard our hearts and care for us, we may never allow ourselves to come out of hiding and be found in Him.

Believe the Lord Will Vindicate You

Perhaps you believe you have made a mistake from which you never will recover. Maybe you tried reaching out to someone and they ripped you off. Perhaps, like Cedric, a spiritual parent has hurt and taken advantage of you, and you feel misunderstood or wrongly accused.

God's Word cautions us away from trying to vindicate ourselves when others accuse us falsely. Instead, we should "drink
the cup" and the Lord will vindicate us as illustrated in Numbers
5:11-22. In the Old Testament, a man who suspected his wife of
adultery brought her to the priest where she was given dirty
water to drink from a cup. If she was guilty, she would get sick
and diseased and become a curse among her people; but if she
was innocent, the Lord would vindicate her. She would be fruitful and bear children. Either way, she had to drink the cup!

God knows our hearts. He knows the truth. It does not
help to try to prove our innocence on our own; He has to do it.
Certainly this does not mean that if someone makes a serious
false accusation against us we should ignore it and hope it will
go away. We can respond in a spirit of humility and address the
false accusation, but then we should lay it down and allow God
to defend us. Our role needs to be one of forgiveness, or we will
harbor resentment.

The Bible says there are two types of ministries before the
throne of God—the ministry of intercession and the "ministry"
of accusation. Jesus intercedes before the Father for us, but the
devil accuses us before the throne. The enemy can never tri-
umph over the Son.

A former co-laborer in church leadership who left our
church several years ago came back to meet with me and one
of my colleagues a few years later. The Lord had spoken to
him and challenged him concerning which of these two "ministries" he was embracing. To his surprise and regret, he realized
that he was participating in a "ministry" of accusation against
me and against the church. It had crippled him and robbed his
joy. The Lord convicted him of his judgmental spirit, and he
sincerely repented. Today, this precious man of God is one
of our personal intercessors. The Lord vindicated me and redeemed our relationship!

If Satan uses someone to lie about us, though it may be tempting to lash out and try to vindicate ourselves, we must simply "drink the cup," in a spirit of humility and forgiveness, believing in faith that the Son will intercede. God is the vindicator.

Believe the Father Will Restore You

Spiritual fathers and mothers in the Body of Christ must grasp this simple, important truth: We need to forgive others just as we want to be forgiven. We must extend mercy to each other and leave the judgment to God (see Luke 6:37). Mercy always triumphs over judgment (see Jas. 2:13)! Mercy is not giving punishment or retribution that is deserved, letting someone off the hook because of love. When we extend mercy to those who have wronged us or made mistakes, they can be restored and rebuilt.

Satan accuses the one struggling: "Can you, as a burned stone, live?"

Jesus answers us loudly and clearly: "Yes, I will restore you and place you back on My wall for service in My kingdom."

We cannot look at our natural circumstances and give up. Our God is a God who forgives and restores burned stones. Mercy illustrates what God is like. Our merciful Lord wants to restore those who have been burned because of sin, by bad role models or by not responding properly to tests the Lord allowed in their lives. He wants us back in fellowship with Him and others.

When we are burned by others through disappointment, unmet expectations or spiritual abuse, we can feel like burned stones. Nevertheless, the Lord is redemptive! He heals burned stones and replaces them on the wall of service.

I know firsthand what this restoration is like. I felt like a burned stone for a period of time while I served as a pastor. Here is how I described what I was going through in my book *House to House*:

During the spring of 1992, I was ready to quit. I felt misunderstood, and I was not sure if it was worth all the hassle. I told LaVerne one day, "If I get kicked in the head one more time (figuratively speaking), I don't know if I can get up again."

As the senior leader of our church, I was frustrated, exhausted and overworked. God had given me a vision to be involved in building the underground church, but in the last few years, we had strayed from that original vision. My immaturity as a leader, lack of training and my own inability to communicate clearly the things that God was showing me led to frustration. In a misguided attempt to please everyone, I was listening to dozens of voices that seemed to be giving conflicting advice and direction. I felt unable to get back on track. I was tired and was encouraged to take a sabbatical.[2]

On that sabbatical, the Lord restored me and gave me new direction. I am grateful that He gave me the grace to continue and to believe again because today I am so fulfilled, replaced on His wall of service. Since that time, the Lord has placed spiritual fathers in my life to encourage me, and learning the incredible value of spiritual fathering has changed my life! It has become my life's mission to be obedient to Him and train others to become spiritual parents. I am so blessed that the Lord would not allow me to quit—I am having the time of my life!

I love this modern-day story of the restoration of a son to his father: A young man named Sawat had disgraced his family and dishonored his father's name. Observe what happened when he refused to listen to the devil's lies anymore:

Sawat had come to Bangkok to escape the dullness of village life. . . . When he first arrived, he had visited a hotel unlike any he had ever seen. Every room had a window facing into the hallway, and in every room sat a girl. . . . That visit began Sawat's adventure into Bangkok's world of prostitution. . . . Soon he was selling opium to customers and propositioning tourists in the hotels. He even went so low as to actually help buy and sell young girls, some of them only nine and ten years old. It was a nasty business, and he was one of the most important of the young "businessmen."

Then the bottom dropped out of his world: He hit a string of bad luck . . . and finally ended up living in a shanty by the city trash pile. Sitting in his little shack, he thought about his family, especially his father, a simple Christian man from a small southern village near the Malaysian border. He remembered his dad's parting words: "I am waiting for you." He wondered whether his father would still be waiting for him after all that he had done to dishonor the family name. . . . Word of Sawat's life-style had long ago filtered back to the village.

Finally, he devised a plan. "Dear father," he wrote, "I want to come home, but I don't know if you will receive me after all that I have done. I have sinned greatly, father. Please forgive me. On Saturday night, I will be on the train that goes through our village. If you are still waiting for me, will you tie a piece of cloth on the po tree in front of our house? (Signed) Sawat."

As the train finally neared the village, he churned with anxiety. . . . Sitting opposite him was a kind stranger who noticed how nervous his fellow passenger had become. Finally, Sawat could stand the pressure no longer. He blurted out his story in a torrent of words. As they entered the village, Sawat said, "Oh sir, I cannot bear to look. Can you watch for me? What if my father will not receive me back?"

Sawat buried his face between his knees. "Do you see it, sir? It's the only house with a po tree."

"Young man, your father did not hang just one piece of cloth. Look! He has covered the whole tree with cloth!" Sawat could hardly believe his eyes. The branches were laden with tiny white squares. In the front yard his old father jumped up and down, joyously waving a piece of white cloth, then ran in halting steps beside the train. When it stopped at the little station, he threw his arms around his son, embracing him with tears of joy. "I've been waiting for you!" he exclaimed.

Sawat's story poignantly parallels Jesus' parable of the Prodigal Son, found in Luke 15:11-24. Christ told of another son who threw his life and money away in a whirlwind of wrong choices and fearfully returned home in the hopes that his father would take him back. He too was met with open arms, and was loved and accepted unconditionally.[3]

The Lord waits with open arms for all those who return to Him. He longs to restore us. His forgiveness and acceptance is always extended. We cannot allow Satan to deceive us, but must instead turn toward our loving Father who runs to meet us as we turn toward home.

Do you know that the Bible says Jesus Christ became a curse for us so that we can be set free from the devil's lies? "Christ redeemed us from the curse of the law by becoming a curse for us . . . The reason the Son of God appeared was to destroy the devil's work" (Gal. 3:13; 1 John 3:8). We can be free from the devil's lies because we are free from the curse. We do not have to live in bondage.

The Lord is a great Redeemer. He is waiting for us to stand up and be used, even if we have made mistakes. Do you know any natural parents who have never made any mistakes? Of course not! God gives grace to parents who place their faith and confidence in Him. We may as well give ourselves room to make some mistakes, because we probably will; the Lord will be there to cover the blunders we make as spiritual parents. We cannot afford to stunt our spiritual growth and languish on the sidelines.

Perhaps you feel you have failed as a natural parent, and that this disqualifies you from being an effective spiritual parent. Nothing could be farther from the truth! The Lord will use your disappointments and failures as a "sword in your hand" against the enemy. You will be the spiritual parent God has called you to be, grounded in a deep humility and trust in the grace and mercy of the Lord.

Likewise, I meet many Christians today who lacked a decent role model for fathering. Although they witnessed dysfunctional, faulty father images while growing up, they allowed the Lord to mold them into godly role models for their own children. They broke from their past. A negative parenting role model is no excuse for us to continue to pass on bad parenting. God is a Father to the fatherless (see Ps. 68:5). He loves us and will teach us to be healthy parents. As we pour our lives into people and love them with the love of Jesus, we will model positive family patterns.

We live in a fallen world, but we were raised with Christ when we were redeemed, bought back by the blood Jesus shed on the cross 2,000 years ago. Jesus came to give us abundant life and to set us free (see John 8:32). Step by step, we reclaim what Satan has stolen from us—in our homes, in our workplaces, at school and beyond. God has a loving plan of redemption for every believer and seeks to accomplish His plan by restoring ordinary people like us.

As those who have been abused, abandoned, burned or broken take a step of faith, trusting the Lord to restore their wounded hearts, He heals them completely and places them back on the wall of service.

Are you ready to believe? If so, begin by taking the first step of restoration.

Steps for Restoration

1. *Unlock the door.* If we hide behind a locked door, attempting to bulletproof ourselves from hurts, we harden our hearts. God wants to expose and free us. How? It's simple. John 8:32 says that when we believe in Christ, we "shall know the truth, and the truth shall make [us] free." Jesus Christ, who is Truth, makes men and women free! We become free from being captives to sin—to our false notions, hurts, mistakes and prejudices that entangle and enslave the soul. Through faith, we unlock the door of our hardened heart and fall into the arms of Him whose yoke is easy and whose burden is light. We trust Jesus to restore our lives.

2. *Stake your claim.* God promised the children of Israel the fertile land of Canaan. It was their land because God promised it to them, but they had to receive it by going in, taking it from their enemies and staking the claim for themselves. The same truth applies to us. We stake our claim on restored and abundant life by taking back the areas of our lives the devil has stolen from us. If the devil has stolen our peace, our joy, our health or our hope, today is our day to claim it back from the enemy! Claim back from the devil the specific areas he has stolen from you.

When we take Him at His Word, the Lord honors His covenant with us!

3. *Receive prayer from a trusted friend.* For help in your restoration process, seek the counsel of a godly friend or spiritual parent. He or she can walk with you as you ask God's forgiveness, receive healing in your emotions and gain the strength to "sin no more" (John 8:11).

4. *Be patient.* The process may not happen overnight. Corrie ten Boom, who experienced life in a Nazi concentration camp, attested to the "ding-dong theory" when it came to finding complete healing. She said that when you ask the Lord to heal and restore you, the devil will try to bring the old emotions of hurt and pain back to you again and again. But like the ding-dong of a church bell that rings loud at first and then grows softer and softer until it finally stops ringing, the hurts will grow more faint and distant as you forgive others and continue to daily claim healing and restoration for your life.

5. *Keep growing.* God is calling you to be a healthy, functional spiritual parent. Even if you have not had a spiritual parent yourself, the Lord will teach you to be a spiritual mentor to the next generation if you keep your eyes on Jesus. Joseph, a man of moral and spiritual strength, was likened to a fruit tree with branches going over the well wall (see Gen. 49:22). The moisture from the well kept the tree watered and bearing fruit. Like Joseph's, your branches will grow abundantly over the wall if you

are constantly watered by the Word of God and the Holy Spirit. When you keep your roots well watered, you will bear fruit for Him in the form of many spiritual children.

Our God is restoring spiritual fathers and mothers to their sons and daughters and gently placing them back on His wall of service. God is calling forth His people who have been burned and broken in these days, and He is healing them and giving them a job to do.

You must find your place on the wall. God loves to use burned stones! If you are a burned stone, receive the grace of God today from your heavenly Father to be made whole through His Son Jesus Christ. God wants to bless you, make you strong and give you a great inheritance of spiritual children.

CHAPTER 8

MULTIPLE MENTORS

 Key: Multiple mentors produce multiple mentors.

Many times God uses more than one spiritual father or mother in a person's life to meet various areas of need. For example, a spiritual parent might mentor someone specifically in the area of healthy family relationships, while another mentor shares her expertise in the area of financial planning and budgeting. (My natural father has served as a mentor to me for years in principles of sound financial management.) Yet another spiritual father or mother may mentor the same spiritual son or daughter in a specific area of Christian ministry.

Even ministry leaders need spiritual moms and dads. In spiritual mentoring, the buck does not stop at any point in the family hierarchy! A pastor's wife may be mentored by another spiritually mature woman, preferably another pastor's wife who understands the needs of someone in the limelight. The senior pastor of a church needs a spiritual father, too, one who might mentor him in sound decision-making and leadership principles.

I have various spiritual fathers to whom I look for spiritual advice and continuing leadership development. Some are theologians, while others have a keen understanding of cross-cultural leadership. I need these fathers in my life if I hope to continue to grow and mature in Christ. I will never outgrow the need for a spiritual mentor.

Another kind of mentor may be someone you have not met personally. For example, you may be mentored by individuals through reading their books or listening to their teaching on CD or DVD. They mentor you by opening their lives through their writing and teaching. One of the reasons I began to write over 12 years ago was that I was so encouraged by others who had gone before me and written about what they had learned and experienced. I realized that I might help others in the same way others had helped me. Today, more than 20 books later, I continue to write about the spiritual truths I have learned through the "school of the Holy Spirit." I pass on to you what I have learned from others and from the Lord.

MANY TYPES OF MENTORS

There are many types of spiritual parents who mentor their protégés in a wide variety of arenas. Nelson Martin, a pastor who serves on the leadership team of DOVE Christian Fellowship in the US, heads up a 24-Hour Prayer Watch for our family of churches. The prayer watch includes prayer generals who oversee prayer warriors who pray for the DCFI family around the clock. Some of these prayer generals guide the prayer warriors under their care by teaching them to pray and hear from God, connecting with them in a prayer mentoring relationship.

Couples can play a vital role in mentoring other couples in their marriage relationships. We have seen gratifying results in DCFI with a successful couple-to-couple marriage mentoring program. The workbook *Called Together*, written by Steve and Mary Prokopchak, is a unique mentoring program designed for counselor mentors to equip engaged couples for marriage and beyond. The material teaches mature couples how to mentor others through varying phases of married life.[1]

Young mothers need older mothers to help them become the wise, capable parents God designed them to be. Experienced professional women can mentor younger professional women toward success. Widows who lost spouses years ago might mentor more-recent widows through their grief and adjustment. Seasoned missionaries can mentor developing missionaries. The term "homogeneous" refers to these "like" kinds of mentoring relationships, and they can be incredibly beneficial.

Business professionals benefit from having other business leaders mentor them in sound practices and ethics. My friend Earl is a successful businessman in our local community. He has told me that the most fulfilling activity in which he participates is meeting with younger business leaders and mentoring them through the potential pitfalls of business and life. He is a spiritual father in the marketplace.

I was thinking about going back into business a few years ago, possibly working on the side as I continued to write and teach in the nations. I have friends involved in ministry leadership who are also involved in business, and it works well for them. To evaluate the pros and cons of such a venture, I sat down with two of my business-leader friends and gave them my proposal. After talking with me and seeking the Lord's direction, they both encouraged me not to do it during this season of my life. They felt strongly that with my present schedule, adding something else to my life would not work. I took their advice and abandoned the potential business venture. I knew that the timing of God is critical, and today, I know I am better for having maintained my focus on leadership in the Body of Christ. It pays to have spiritual fathers in the marketplace.

A few years ago I was seated next to a businessman on a flight to Seattle. We struck up a conversation and he asked me what I do for a living. I told him that I'm involved in Christian leadership training and that I write and teach on mentoring.

He, in turn, told me that he is in a management role in one of the major airplane manufacturing corporations in America. And then he said an amazing thing. He told me that his corporation had recently come to the realization that they had lost an entire generation's worth of brain trust in their company. They had neglected to mentor younger workers to understand the strategic plan and vision for the company. When the leadership realized their near-catastrophic mistake, they immediately decided that no one in management would advance in the company until they were actively engaged in mentoring the next generation.

Sometimes corporations use biblical truths to run their businesses, while we in the Church continue to live by our misguided religious traditions. But this is changing. God is restoring the biblical truth of spiritual fathering and mothering to His people, and in some places He is using the corporate world to do it.

Whatever their area of expertise, the Lord wants to use mature, knowledgeable believers to grow you into a thriving follower of Jesus, and He wants to use *your* passion and know-how to mentor the next generation.

NOT JUST MULTIPLE MENTORS— *MULTIPLICATION* OF MENTORS!

When our youngest daughter, Leticia, was in her senior year of high school, her school offered a program that allowed students to explore career possibilities by accompanying someone as he or she went through a normal day in the workplace. As the students followed the nurses, journalists, bankers, scientists, engineers, technicians and administrative professionals who served as their mentors, they got a professional's-eye look at that job and its workplace environment. While they were provided with information about various career paths, resources and programs, "shadowing," or exposing students to different professions through up-close and personal contact, was found to be the most valuable way to jump start students' thinking about the limitless possibilities for their futures.

By shadowing mentors in their daily lives, a spiritual son or daughter learns the basics of spiritual parenting naturally, quickly and easily. Up-close and personal contact is the start of a powerful legacy—the possibilities are limitless. (Though we must remember that legacies come after the fact. If we dwell on the end results, it's too easy to get overwhelmed!)

Spiritual fathering and mothering is a process, and sometimes a long one! But as "each one fathers one," our efforts are multiplied. The unique teaching methods of Dr. Frank Laubach can give us a glimpse of just how greatly they can be multiplied:

Dr. Frank Laubach's epitaph ascribes to him the following title: "The man who taught the world to read." Dr. Laubach popularized the phrase "each one teach one." Via his simple four-word strategy of teaching one person to read under the condition that each would teach another to read, several million people have now experienced the thrill and freedom of reading for the first time. The chain continues to this day, long after his death. Today the Laubach Method has more than eighty thousand volunteers worldwide.

Pause for sixty seconds and try to imagine the implications of this: You mentor 12, who mentor 12, equaling 144!

who mentor 12, equaling 1,728!
who mentor 12, equaling 20,736!
who mentor 12, equaling 248,832!
who mentor 12, equaling 2,985,984!

Is an unbroken chain of mentors realistic? Probably not! But the point is clear. Even if only a small fraction of protégés follow through by mentoring someone else, a significant difference will be made in the number of leaders in the next centuries—or until the Lord returns![2]

It's obvious that the multiplication potential of spiritual parenting is phenomenal! Quite naturally, in spiritual family relationships, spiritual babies grow into young men or women and finally become spiritual fathers or mothers. And before you know it, a spiritual legacy is created. The explosive result demonstrated above is the natural multiplication that happens when each successive generation takes up the mantle of spiritual mentoring. But the process multiplies with exponential force only when each generation refuses to wait until they are spiritual giants before they become spiritual fathers and mothers. They know that you can *have* a spiritual father and *be* a spiritual father simultaneously (and in fact, that's how the process works best!). As each new generation steps up to the plate, spiritual fathers and mothers are constantly multiplied and released.

PART III

BEING A SPIRITUAL MENTOR

CHAPTER 9

THE JESUS MODEL

 Key: Mentors initiate, build and release.

When I was a young leader, I felt I needed to be everyone's friend on an equal basis. As you might expect, I soon found there was not enough of me to go around! As I prayed and pondered Jesus' relationships with His disciples, it became clear to me that Jesus worked within the same constraints we are bound by: He could effectively be in close mentoring relationships with only a small number of people. The level of His relational investment did not depend on how long He had known His followers or on their expectations; He clearly heard from His heavenly Father regarding the disciples He should spend the most time with. Jesus did that which His Father led Him to do (see John 5:19) and thereby gave us the perfect mentoring model: to value all people, but to develop deep friendships only with a few.

God created us to need others and to be needed by them. Jesus was God but also fully human, and He had the same relational needs we have. A mentor will have relationships of varying levels of friendship and intimacy, and to sort these out, it helps to understand the spheres of relationship Jesus modeled and to apply these to spiritual mentoring. Jesus had an inner circle of friends: Peter, James and John. He spent much quality time with these three and John in particular. Beyond this tight-knit circle,

Jesus closely mentored the 12 disciples, with whom He traveled day to day. Beyond those friendships, He was in relationship with the 72 disciples He sent out "two by two ahead of him to every town and place where he was about to go" (Luke 10:1). Lastly, Jesus was a spiritual father to the 120 faithful believers who waited in the Upper Room for the promised Holy Spirit. Jesus also ministered to the multitudes, but this was most often done in the company and with the assistance of His friends and protégés.

Jesus knew that Kingdom values are caught more than taught, so He *initiated* close relationships with followers who were ready to catch, and spent the majority of His time *building*— nurturing and preparing the Twelve to fulfill the Lord's purpose for their lives. And when they were ready (and probably before they *felt* ready!), He *released* them to live out the Kingdom values they had caught and to continue His mission of initiating, building and releasing even more disciples, who would, in turn, all do the same. From the Sermon on the Mount to the Sea of Galilee, from the Temple gates to the Garden of Gethsemane, day in and day out, Jesus modeled healthy and effective spiritual mentoring. He fished, prayed, wept and rejoiced with the disciples until they could follow His example and mentor many more people in the kingdom of God.

When Jesus trained His disciples, He didn't do it sitting on a hill somewhere, lecturing them for three years. He taught them through real-life experiences as they traveled from place to place. They actively learned, by Jesus' example and demonstration, how to be a part of the kingdom of God. The disciples witnessed God's power and compassion firsthand when they came to Jesus with bread, which He multiplied to feed a hungry crowd. They learned to discern the true from the false when Jesus exposed the scribes and Pharisees in their false piety and self-righteousness and affirmed the true generosity of the widow with two pennies. Their fingers learned to heal the sick, to give sight to the blind and to bring the lame to their feet by watching the caring Master touch those who needed God's hand. Their hearts were trained to love the oppressed, the poor and the little children when they saw the heart of Jesus moved and His eyes filled with tears again and again.

After three years the disciples were not perfect, but Jesus believed in them enough to entrust the Church to their care when the time came for Him to return to the Father. He knew they had caught the heart of the kingdom of God.

FOLLOWING THE MODEL OF JESUS

At its most basic, a spiritual mentor's task is to follow the Jesus model of *initiating, building* and *releasing*. Spiritual parents invite their spiritual children into relationship (*initiate*), nurture and guide them (*build*) and *release* them to mentor others.

Jesus *initiated* His close relationships, choosing 12 friends from 72 of His followers to be His key disciples. He had known them, walked with them and watched their lives, but now it was time to get serious, so He prayed all night and chose the Twelve. In the same way, the persons whom the Lord may call us to mentor in a closer relationship will probably be those we are in some type of friendship with already.

Taking our cue from Jesus, spiritual parents must take the *initiative* and get to know our spiritual son or daughter well. To do so, we need to spend time with him or her, because getting to know someone takes intentional effort! We can start by spending time together doing something we both enjoy, such as fishing, scrapbooking, going to a sports game or baking cookies. We might talk about where we came from, our thoughts about our current status and our hopes and dreams for the future.

When a solid foundation of relationship is laid, it's time to *build*. The goal of spiritual parents must be to equip and invest in their children to increase their effectiveness for the Kingdom, but this can take many different shapes. If you are mentoring someone for ministry, take them along to the hospital when you visit a sick member from your small group, or participate with them in an evangelism outreach in your community. Let them see you serve using your gifts and knowledge, and help them grow in these areas, too. If you are mentoring a parent, invite him or her to spend time with you and your children to watch you discipline and shepherd them, or tell stories about raising your kids. Be honest about your mistakes and challenges, high points and low moments. Pray with them when they struggle. If you are mentoring a student, be available to help them succeed with their school work, and to answer their confused questions when they encounter ideas that seem to contradict God's Word. Whatever the particular situation, nurture and encourage your protégé to draw closer to the Father, to increase in knowledge and wisdom, and to spread their wings in boldness.

Over the course of time, as you remain sensitive to God's leading, you will know when it is time to *release* your son or daughter into the next stage: parenting their own spiritual children. After a time of watching Jesus minister to others, the disciples were released by Jesus to do the same thing.

Many discipleship systems today are stagnant and limited and don't actually accomplish making disciples. A pastor is paid to "feed the flock" and the people get their money's worth in good sermons and great programs. Too often, because he is one man doing the work of everyone, the pastor burns out and moves on to another church, and the people never fulfill their calling in Christ to become equipped and empowered by His Spirit and then released as disciple-ministers themselves. They never become spiritual fathers and mothers. We must change our focus on programs and our spectator mentality to a focus on empowering and fathering people in spiritual family settings with a multiplication mentality.

If we don't change our focus and begin to release new generations of spiritual parents, the Church will continue to overflow with "emotional and spiritual orphans," according to Floyd McClung in his book *The Father Heart of God*:

> So many people are orphaned, not just from their physical parents, but from any kind of healthy spiritual or emotional heritage. The church is also filled with spiritual orphans. Either they have accepted Jesus Christ but have not been nurtured in their faith, or because of some failure on their own or someone else's part they have not yet become a part of a spiritual family. These people desperately need pastoral care. They need to be taught God's Word, to be counseled with sound biblical principles, and to be encouraged and exhorted by someone mature in the faith. They need a spiritual father or mother who can help them grow in the Lord.
>
> Others need to be "reparented"—that is, given the kind of example that only a wise, stable mother or father figure can provide. If proper parenting was missing during a person's developmental years, whether physically or spiritually or both, he or she needs someone to provide an example.
>
> Being a father or mother in the Lord is not limited to those who are pastors or spiritual leaders. There is also a very crucial need for other spiritually mature, caring people to act as "fathers" and "mothers" to other believers.
>
> By their very presence, they minister to those around them because of their maturity and depth in God. We need to turn loose these "moms and dads" in

the church to be who they are. By being available, having time for people, and having an open home, their lives can be instruments of healing and love.[1]

When you sense your spiritual children are ready, it's time for on-the-job training! Ask for their input in a variety of situations. What would they do differently if they were you? What are their observations? How can these observations be turned into life or ministry principles? As you observe your spiritual son or daughter testing what they have learned, it is important to evaluate them and give feedback, including areas for suggested growth and improvement. This give-and-take allows them to apply and adapt to their own situation what they have seen you do.

Listen attentively and respectfully to your spiritual son or daughter tell you about the "new" successful idea you have used a dozen times. Help them analyze the reasons when the idea fails or succeeds. Mistakes will be made—you can count on it!—but fledgling spiritual parents need to make their own mistakes and learn to deal with the consequences. Remember: Our God is a God of second chances. If Jonah could receive a second chance, so can they! Encourage your protégé to press on. Share with them feelings of fear and inadequacy you have felt many times. Be honest and vulnerable, and they will learn to do the same for the next generation.

Give assignments to your spiritual son or daughter when it's clear from your conversations and observations that they are ready. If you are going to pray for a sick person, for instance, invite your son or daughter to tag along. Then the next time there is a need for prayer, ask your son or daughter to lead out while you are there for support. Start with small things and increase to greater responsibilities. Eventually your spiritual children will take their own spiritual children with them to pray.

Get the picture? That's how spiritual children are released.

BUILD RELATIONSHIPS

In the Old Testament, God's people consisted of 12 tribes and a multitude of clans and families known corporately as the children of Israel. Through these family relational connections, God demonstrated the importance of generational inheritance, which is passed from father to son. Receiving this inheritance, which was first promised to Abraham and then passed on to his descendants, depended on the flow of blessing from generation to generation.

In similar fashion, Jesus mentored His disciples to grow His Church based on mentoring believers in spiritual families. The Early Church knew the importance of relational connection. The Scriptures tell us that God's people gathered at the Temple and met in small groups to minister to each other: "So continuing daily with one accord in the temple, and breaking bread from house to house, they ate their food with gladness and simplicity of heart, praising God and having favor with all the people. And the Lord added to the church daily those who were being saved" (Acts 2:46-47).

The Early Church followed the disciples' example of spiritual parenting by meeting "house to house" to experience spiritual family life to its fullest. These assemblies were vibrant and alive. The believers had a deep love for each other, and joyfulness and generosity were the outstanding hallmarks of their relationships. They sold their possessions to provide for the needs of others. They remained steadfast in the apostles' teachings, learned to pray with results, rejoiced when persecuted and were willing to die for their faith. They were held in high honor by others who observed their lifestyle.

Relationships were the key to the explosive growth of the kingdom of God in the Early Church. In these house fellowship groups, spiritual families were raised and multiplied. Through small groups meeting in homes, members were nurtured, equipped to serve and could easily use their spiritual gifts to build each other up to become like Christ. They met together with joy and love for each other, and new people were continually added to the Church family. Who wouldn't want the vibrant connections these believers exemplified?

This kind of New Testament Church life, in which people were in relationship with each other and their God, is a model that today's spiritual parents must imitate. Healthy families have parents who take their God-given responsibility as fathers and mothers to their children very seriously. John the apostle challenged the early believers to "practice loving each other, for love comes from God and those who are loving and kind show that they are children of God, and they are getting to know him better" (1 John 4:7, *TLB*). Living in close relationships with others, which was ordained by God for the children of Israel and then replicated in the close friendships of Jesus with His disciples and their parenting of the next generations, reflects our understanding of God's design and intention for His people.

This small-group, family-like model is springing up in all types of churches in nearly every nation of the world. Not too long ago I was in Brazil, where I spent time with a pastor friend who recently started a new church. Eight years after he began, there are more than 21,000 people in the church, all involved in small groups in which each one is mentored by spiritual fathers and mothers. God is calling His Church back to the simplicity of spiritual family life, and the Church is growing just as it did in its earliest days.

The Bible says that we are living stones for God's use in building His house: "You also, as living stones, are being built up a spiritual house . . ." (1 Pet. 2:5). We, as redeemed people in whom God now resides, are "living stones." We are built together with the mortar of God-ordained relationships into a spiritual house. Without these strong connections, we soon fall apart and lay as useless rubble on the ground.

Sadly, today there are many living stones lying useless on a pile. Many Christians, instead of being cemented to other believers in family-type relationships, are haphazardly thrown on a heap as they assemble once a week to hear a sermon and sing some songs, and then leave without any real, bonding interaction. Instead of being the family God has called them to be, they come together every Sunday morning in a large gathering of relative strangers. Rather than experiencing the day-to-day love of a true spiritual family, they experience a weekly family reunion.

There's a huge difference between the vibrant life of an immediate family and an extended family getting together for a reunion. When long-lost relatives come together for a reunion, they present their best face to the larger family, who don't see them often enough to know better. They swap stories and testimonies about their accomplishments and extol their successes, like the fantastic goal Jeremy scored on the soccer team and Meagan becoming an honor student. But much of this hoopla, while worth celebrating, is superficial.

Real, immediate family know about the struggles, because they are there day after day. They know that Jeremy worked long and hard to reach his present caliber of soccer play and had a major setback when he broke his leg in three places. They know that Meagan had to overcome a learning disability and apply herself to diligent study in order to attain the distinction of becoming an honor student. Real, immediate family know each other inside out. They see the good, the bad and the ugly, and they still love each other and work as a unit to encourage each member. We can be ourselves in a family. There is no test to pass; we are included simply because *we are family*.

Likewise, a spiritual family readily shares both the struggles and the triumphs in transparent relationships, with spiritual parents to guide and nurture their spiritual children.

A few years ago in the Pacific Northwest, I met Sam, an airline pilot, and his wife, Janice. Sam grew up with a religious background but had been turned off by church. When his neighbor, Duane, invited him to attend a small-group meeting in their home, Sam at first declined. He wanted nothing to do with Christianity. The Christians he knew were self-righteous hypocrites, consumed with making sure others followed all the rules and regulations.

But Duane and the guys from the group persisted in connecting with Sam. When they saw that he was adding a room to his house, they offered to help. Sometime between hammering nails and laying down carpet, Sam's perception of Christians began to change for the better. These guys were real. They didn't spout a lot of overdone Christian clichés. They admitted their weaknesses and clearly "walked their talk."

Eventually Sam and Janice both gave their lives to the Lord, and the men and women in the small group next door became their spiritual mentors. As Sam gave up his bad habits one at a time, the men never condemned him, but supported him as a family would. Today, Sam and Janice parent their own spiritual family of growing believers.

Duane, as a spiritual mentor, and the guys in his small group understood the importance of building relationships and making connections. They followed the example set by Jesus, and the family of God continues to grow.

SEE POTENTIAL

Recognizing the undeveloped traits, gifts and abilities of a son or daughter is a spiritual father's or mother's responsibility. Jesus modeled this as well. He changed Simon's name to Peter, which means "rock." Peter didn't act like a solid, stable foundation stone when he fell asleep in the Garden or denied Jesus three times, but the Lord knew Peter's heart and saw his potential. The apostle later grew into the rock Jesus predicted he would become, and encouraged his spiritual children, as we have seen, to become living stones in the same way.

Although spiritual parents cannot predict their son's or daughter's future, they can help them set goals for tomorrow and develop their gifts today. If both mentor and protégé are diligent about honing these gifts, God will be able to use them to serve Him and others more fully in the future.

It should be noted that Jesus did not nag Peter to grow up, even after He called him a rock. Ephesians 6:4 offers advice to fathers, both natural and spiritual, to guide their children (which includes seeing their potential) without unduly criticizing them: "And you, fathers, do not provoke your children to wrath, but bring them up in the training and admonition of the Lord." Children will not reach their potential if parents demoralize them with unrealistic expectations or constant criticisms. A spiritual mentor should not be too quick to correct his protégé's mistakes or expect too much too soon. Although honesty is important and a mentor should not overlook a fault if it hinders their spiritual child's walk with the Lord, spiritual parents should be slow to barge in and correct.

Sometimes a mentor will see a weakness and realize that the best way for the son or daughter to overcome it is to discover it themselves. In that case, the mentor simply ensures that he is available to help process and deal with the weakness when it surfaces to the protégé's attention. Instead of pointing out the fault too quickly, the parent prays for and builds up the spiritual child with encouraging words, refusing to dishearten the growing protégé with nagging and criticism.

Nurture Trust

Trust is the cornerstone of a successful mentoring relationship, which grows in small increments and accumulates over time. Trust begins when the spiritual son or daughter is assured of the mentor's love. I heard someone once say that God calls us to a higher love than the world demands, a love that does not wait for people to change. Spiritual fathers and mothers accept their sons and daughters as they are, even as they gently encourage them to grow. An environment must be provided that allows them to be themselves without fear of judgment or impatience on the mentor's part. A commitment to the confidentiality of discussions is also a necessity. Only then can trust blossom.

In His day-to-day life, Jesus modeled the Christlike character traits for His followers that we should seek to emulate: compassion, wisdom, honesty, purity, and so on. He knew that spontaneous interaction is important when nurturing trust. Because growth and maturity are more caught than taught, informal exchange and contact model the kingdom of God by showing how Christianity works in real life.

A spiritual son should witness how his mentor functions in his everyday world and witness firsthand how his spiritual father deals with life's quirky situations—the good, the bad and the ugly. A spiritual mother should allow her spiritual daughter to observe her in real-life family relationships—how she handles crisis situations, such as when her teenager comes in past curfew or when her husband is working late *again*. Mentors can invite their spiritual son and daughter over for meals and make them feel a part of their family. They can hang out together, golf together, shop together, eat together, fish together, bake together, weed the garden together or attend a sporting event together. As time is spent rubbing shoulders with each other, trust slowly blooms and bears fruit.

BE AVAILABLE

Jesus was completely approachable and fully accessible to His disciples for three years, and they grew spiritually mature under His tutelage. When a spiritual mentor follows the model of Jesus, they make themselves accessible and available to their protégé. Today's society, especially in the Western world, encourages us to be individualistic and selfish with our time. We fill our calendars to the maximum with work-related tasks, and we're sure to pencil in generous time slots for recreation and taking care of number one. A loving spiritual parent selflessly refuses to fall into this egocentric trap.

A spiritual mentoring relationship is marked by its liberality because spiritual mentors give of their time generously and sacrificially just as Jesus did with His disciples. With an open heart and hand, they purposefully take their spiritual children under their wing. It is not always comfortable to make oneself available at 2 A.M. for a crisis phone call, but a spiritual father graciously takes it in stride because he loves his son.

According to family counselor John M. Drescher, our children need our time. He tells the story of a son who was watching his father polish the car. After observing the time and careful attention lavished on the automobile, eventually the boy asked, "Dad, your car's worth a lot, isn't it?"

"Yes," his dad replied, "it cost a lot. It pays to take care of it. When I trade the car in, it will be worth more if I take care of it."

After some silence the son said, "I guess I'm not worth very much, am I?"[2]

When a spiritual father spends time with his son, the son knows that he is worth a great deal. And a spiritual mother knows that when she invests her life in nurturing her daughter, the daughter will grow up to be spiritually productive.

On the flipside, red flags should go up if a spiritual son or daughter expects too much of his or her mentor's time and energy. Expecting a mentor to be available whenever and wherever the protégé has a need is unrealistic. The amount of time spent together in a mentoring relationship should be more or less determined in advance.

If a mentor's kids say things like, "Dad, why is Ryan here all the time?" or a husband complains that his wife's spiritual daughter gets more attention than he does, these are warning signs that the protégé is expecting too much of his or her mentor's time. Mentors cannot be at the beck and call of their spiritual children's whims to the detriment of their own families. Mentoring *is* a commitment of time and energy, but options should be explored to make *efficient* and *effective* use of time. The quality of time spent together is more important than the quantity.

IMPART!

When Jesus shared with His disciples what He considered most important in preparation for His death, He spoke these words:

> As the Father has loved me, so have I loved you. Now remain in my love. If you obey my commands, you will remain in my love, just as I have obeyed my Father's commands and remain in his love. I have told you this so that my joy may be in you and that your joy may be complete. My command is this: Love each other as I have loved you. Greater love has no one than this, that he lay down his life for his friends. You are my friends if you do what I command. I no longer call you servants, because a servant does not know his master's business. Instead, I have called you friends, for everything that I learned from my Father I have made known to you (John 15:9-15).

Jesus had passed on everything the Father had given Him to the disciples assembled in the upper room. It was His joy to impart to His friends everything He had to give.

Spiritual parents will experience the true joy of mentoring when they take what they have and impart it to their spiritual children. *To impart* means "to give another what one is or has." Through a spiritual mentor's teaching and influence, an impartation of everything the mentor is willing to give is conferred on their spiritual sons and daughters.

Natural parents want to see their children grow into maturity. They teach them by example because they know if they do a good job, their lineage will be prosperous and healthy. The parenting process has at its core the intention of raising healthy children who can produce more productive and healthy children.

This is also the heart's cry of spiritual fathers and mothers. Their goal is for their children to reach their full potential as men and women of God. In a spiritual mentoring relationship, all this takes place in an atmosphere of patient love and acceptance, without judgment or fear of rejection. It happens naturally and easily by example and modeled behavior as spiritual parents initiate, build and release their family of spiritual children, imparting everything they have to give.

This is mentoring in the way of Jesus.

A SPIRITUAL MENTOR'S JOB DESCRIPTION

 Key: Develop the kind of mentoring relationship your protégé needs.

Les is on the pastoral team of one of our DCFI churches in Pennsylvania. He says he is indebted to a man who encouraged him when he encountered Christ as a young adult:

> My life was dramatically changed when I came to Christ. I started attending a church, but a few months later, after attending every church meeting and activity I could find, I still felt disconnected and insecure in my faith. Everyone else seemed to have it all together. Sure, I was learning a lot and had made many friends, but initially I had no one I really trusted to ask those soul-searching questions that nagged and threatened to destroy my newly found faith. I really was at a loss to know how to apply the truth of God's Word to my life.
>
> If it had not been for a 77-year-old spiritual father from my church who took a special interest in me, I would have probably thrown in the towel. But this elderly man patiently answered my searching questions

and sacrificially devoted hours explaining the Scriptures to me. In addition, he spent time just being my friend. Through the mentoring of my first spiritual dad, I was firmly planted in God's Word and grew spiritually strong.

I am convinced that this man and the subsequent spiritual fathers the Lord brought into my life were key factors in my maturing process in Christ. I clearly remember the night one of my spiritual fathers called me on the phone and asked me to go with him to pray for a sick man from our church. I had never done this before. As we walked into the man's home, my spiritual father handed me a bottle of oil so we could pray for him, anointing him according to James chapter 5. I opened the bottle and dumped the whole bottle of oil on him. The poor guy had oil running down over his face onto his shoulders. I almost drowned him!

On the way home that evening, my spiritual father gently advised me, "Lester, next time, go a bit light on the oil!" He treated me like a son and loved me unconditionally even when I made mistakes. I learned by practical demonstration the importance of training others by example.

These caring father-son relationships carried me through my first years as a Christian. My spiritual fathers passed the baton to me, depositing in me a desire to be a father to others. I am so grateful.[1]

Les determined he would take the biblical challenge to give his life to others, following his spiritual fathers' examples. Today, Les is a pastor who challenges all believers to demonstrate the love of God in action by developing vital relationships with younger Christians, and in doing so, perpetuates a legacy of spiritual parenting.

DIFFERENT KINDS OF MENTORING

Les's very first spiritual father focused on grounding him in the Word and answering his questions about what living a Christian life truly is. One of his later mentors helped Les develop his gifts and spread his ministry wings. Like Les's different spiritual fathers, mentors may be involved in different types of mentoring relationships with their protégés, including mentoring as disciplers, coaches, teachers, counselors, and so on. Let's look at a few of these kinds of mentoring relationships.

Discipler

If a spiritual son or daughter is a new Christian, a mentor will want to disciple this young Christian. That means spending time studying the Bible together, answering questions and praying together. The mentor's role in this relationship is to ground the new spiritual son or daughter in the basics of the Christian faith, laying the foundation for a fruitful life of following Jesus.

The first few years after our cell-based church started, we discovered the pressing need for a basic biblical foundation course to help mentors disciple new believers. To meet that need, I wrote 12 books titled *The Biblical Foundation Series* that presented basic Christian foundations that could be taught systematically from the Scriptures.[2] They are geared especially for spiritual parenting relationships, complete with teaching outlines and questions broken down into increments of time. The response we got from these Christian doctrine books was amazing. Within a few short years, over 300,000 of the books were distributed throughout the Body of Christ. God's people are hungry for practical discipling tools to use in spiritual fathering and mothering relationships.

A study like this that helps to build firm Christian faith is an excellent tool to use in a spiritual mentoring relationship for younger Christians. New believers need to become grounded in

God's Word. Discipler-mentors are those who relationally reach out to their protégés to teach them biblical truths. They take responsibility for maintaining accountability with the protégés until they grow to maturity, become disciples themselves and go on to disciple others.

Coach

Coaching is often described as helping people clarify their goals and develop strategies for achieving those goals. As a coach, a mentor shares his or her skills, knowledge and expertise to help his or her protégé grow in a particular direction, guiding them through the process of setting and reaching goals. Coaching is goal-oriented and may focus on almost any area of life, such as business, career, family, health, personal growth, spirituality and financial responsibility. A wise coach will also help his or her protégé to develop and sharpen their ministry skills and become more effective. Coach-mentors help protégés gain the results they want in the way they want, and build on their strengths and resources.

Teacher

A spiritual son or daughter may need mentoring in areas as diverse as leadership development, cross-cultural evangelism or conflict resolution. Teacher-mentors are those who can organize information and present it so that their protégés learn it rapidly. This information can be imparted in a training course, a small group or person to person. Regardless of the setting, a teacher-mentor challenges his protégée to use the information and make it relevant to his or her life.

Counselor

The central focus of a counselor-mentor is timely counsel and perspective for the protégé's life. These wise mentors act as sounding boards for their spiritual son or daughter to process new ideas or difficult situations, and they impart hope when the protégé's world seems overwhelming. Counselor-mentors listen carefully and help their protégés avoid making serious misjudgments as they work through issues in their past or present. They give specific advice for specific situations.

Of course, the mentoring relationship can be all these rolled up into one. I have had mentoring relationships in which I helped cultivate a new believer's faith in Christ, coached him in family and career development, trained him in leadership development and imparted advice. I was a discipler, coach, teacher and counselor at different points in the relationship, according to what my spiritual son needed.

Group Mentors

Some spiritual mentors maintain a one-on-one mentoring relationship with their spiritual sons and daughters and also mentor them in a small-group setting, where additional protégés meet to pray and study the Bible together. It can be beneficial for spiritual children to have healthy interaction in a group setting with others while a spiritual parent observes and trains them. A group, however, cannot take the place of a person-to-person relationship that occurs when a father sits down with his son face to face and intentionally takes the time to listen and really sense what he is feeling.

Please note that small groups are especially effective when the time comes to release your spiritual children. In groups, everyone has an opportunity to be spiritual fathers and mothers and train the next generation.

Reverse Mentors

I want to mention one other type of mentor in this section who has been coined a "reverse mentor." Reverse mentoring is a twist

on traditional mentoring, given that it is the younger protégé
that teaches the older person something new or valuable rather
than the other way around. The relationship involves both giving and getting feedback, but this time it is the older person
who is the one tapping into the wisdom of the young.

The concept of "reverse mentoring" first gained widespread
attention in the late 1990s when a former chairman of GE
instructed several hundred of his top managers to work with
younger employees to learn about the Internet.[3] He realized
that the younger generation was light years ahead of the older
generation in their knowledge of technology. The outgrowth
these kinds of relationships forged was quite productive and
the sharing of knowledge seemed to work both ways.

In his book *Off-Road Disciplines*, Earl Creps encourages the
older generation to go "off road" and develop reverse-mentoring
relationships. He says they are "a very specific form of friendship in which the junior instructs the senior, not as a replacement
for other forms of mentoring but as an essential complement
to them." Creps goes on to say:

> Reverse mentoring opens up the possibility of a rela-
> tionship in which both participants simultaneously
> teach and learn, each making the other an adopted peer.
> "As iron sharpens iron, so one man sharpens another"
> (Proverbs 27:17). Strictly one-way mentoring (upward
> or downward) resembles iron sharpening wood: all the
> power is on the side of the person whittling the other . . .
> but with iron on both sides, each can be sharpened or
> conformed into the image of Christ through the work
> of the Spirit in the relationship. A reciprocal relation-
> ship between young and old holds the potential for
> a . . . partnership . . . in a way that no other method
> can produce.[4]

For example, young people have a lot to teach the older generation about computers, iPods, text messaging and Xboxes because they grew up with these technologies and are much more proficient using them. Right now, my tech-savvy son-in-law is reverse mentoring me in computer skills. Whenever I want my computer to perform a task I don't know how to make it perform, he comes to the rescue.

Some of Paul's instructions to Timothy seem to have reverse mentoring in view, such as, "Do not rebuke an older man harshly, but exhort him as if he were your father. Treat younger men as brothers, older women as mothers, and younger women as sisters" (1 Tim. 5:1-2). Paul knew that when generations work together, they realize how much they need each other. Their different perspectives allow a sharing of knowledge that would never happen otherwise.

SPIRITUAL MENTORING FUNDAMENTALS

Whatever shape your mentoring relationship takes, there are a few basics that apply. Let's take a look at these non-negotiables.

Praying

Prayer must be woven into the very fabric of the mentoring relationship. Praying for your spiritual son or daughter will wrap them in the Lord's protection and increase your sensitivity to their spiritual growth. Spiritual parenting cannot be just another item on your to-do list. Christians have enough meetings to attend and things to do already! Developing a spiritual mentoring relationship must be something the Lord imparts to you personally, and it must be birthed in prayer. Pray initially that the Lord will lead you to the right relationship, and then pray diligently every day for your spiritual son or daughter. Remember that "the effective, fervent prayer of a righteous man [or woman] avails much" (Jas. 5:16).

Paul wrote in Galatians 4:19 that he labored "in the pains of childbirth" for the Galatian church for Christ to be formed in them. Much of his "labor" was in prayer for those believers. He invested a lot of time in these Christians, whom he affectionately called his "children," and he expected that each one would grow up spiritually strong.

Job rose early every morning and offered a sacrifice for each of his children (see Job 1:5). Jesus was the ultimate mentor, and He prayed for His spiritual children so that they would not fail. In the Gospel of Luke we read that He prayed for Simon Peter out of His special concern for his spirit. Jesus knew that Peter was about to deny Him: "Simon, Simon, Satan has asked to sift you as wheat. But I have prayed for you, Simon, that your faith may not fail" (Luke 22:31-32). Jesus is at the right hand of the Father interceding not only for the world in general but also for us individually (see Rom. 8:34).

Ibrahim Omondi, who oversees DCFI churches in Kenya and serves as a spiritual father to other church leaders in East Africa, describes how prayer with a spiritual father brought him to a place of spiritual maturity: "Those who had discipled me as a young Christian had long moved out of my life. I was left on my own until at a Bible school, I met an elderly professor who asked if I could pray with him regularly. Our weekly prayer meetings soon took on the form of a father-son relationship. I loved it. I recognized what I had missed throughout my Christian walk. I was able to open up in prayer. The deepest secrets of my life found no hiding place. I felt a new sense of security, love and deep humility."

We must pray specific prayers for our spiritual children. Pray that they will run to God and hunger for God's Word. Pray that they will learn to resist temptation and flee from it.

Hearing from God

Not only should spiritual parents diligently pray for their pro-tégés, but they should also teach them to hear from God for themselves. Spiritual sons and daughters will grow to maturity as they learn to hear and discern God's voice.

Jesus told His disciples one day that sheep follow the shep-herd "because they know his voice" (John 10:4). How do they know his voice? Because they spend time with him, know him and have learned from experience that he can be trusted. In the same way, to hear God's voice clearly, we must have a growing love relationship with God and trust Him. It's that simple. The better we get to know God, the better we will recognize His voice.

The Bible is filled with examples of common and ordinary people who heard the voice of a mighty God. Adam and Eve walked and talked with God in the Garden of Eden. The Lord startled Moses from within a flaming bush in the desert when He called him to deliver the Israelites out of the bondage of Egypt. God advised Joshua to be strong and courageous, and gave David fresh strategies for each battle against his enemies. Through the angel Gabriel, the Lord told Mary she would be the mother of Jesus. God affirmed Jesus at His baptism through a voice from heaven, and Paul was totally transformed by the Lord's voice on the Damascus road. When God's people hear His voice, lives are changed.

God delights in revealing Himself to us. He promises to answer if we call on Him: "Call to me and I will answer you and tell you great and unsearchable things you do not know" (Jer. 33:3). When we pray, we engage ourselves in conversation with God and God responds.

On the other hand, we need to share with our protégé that everyone at one time or another struggles to hear God's voice. We want to do what the Lord wants us to do and we know we serve a living God who speaks to us, yet we all struggle when we do not hear as clearly as we would like. It may seem as if we are trying to tune in to a weak radio signal with a lot of static. Despite our trouble hearing, God wants to speak to us even more than we desire to hear from Him.

Other times we think we have heard the Lord's voice and respond to it only to find that we were wrong. Instead of pressing in to find out how and why we "missed it," we may hesitate to step out in faith the next time. Though we may wish God would send a 10-foot angel dressed in white so that we have no doubt it is His voice we are hearing, I believe He often teaches us through our stumbling attempts of trial and error.

Even Jesus' disciples did not always recognize His voice. When Jesus joined two of His disciples on the road to Emmaus and began to talk to them, they didn't recognize Him even though they had walked with Him, talked with Him and eaten meals with Him for the past three years (see Luke 24:13-32). Perhaps they were so immersed in the details of the dark events of the past few days that they couldn't hear clearly. I think there is a good chance, however, that they did not see Jesus because they simply did not expect to see Him. He appeared to them in an unfamiliar form, at an unexpected time and their ears remained closed.

Before we criticize these disciples, we must ask ourselves, "How often do we experience the same loss of hearing today?" Could it be that the Lord sometimes speaks to us in ways that are unfamiliar to us and we don't recognize His voice? We lament that we can't hear Him speak, but in reality He has been speaking all along. Could it be that our understanding of hearing His voice is limited? Maybe we have preconceived ideas how God will speak or not speak to us, and they keep us from hearing God when He speaks.

I'm convinced that we should not get too selective about the method in which the Lord speaks to us. Instead, we should stay open for the Lord to speak to us any way He desires. He is speaking to us every day in ways we may often miss. The Bible says, "For God does speak—now one way, now another—though man may not perceive it" (Job 33:14).

The Bible gives us many clues to hearing God's voice. Our ears must be tuned to hear Him. The Lord has an enormous range of options for speaking to us. He may use the inner witness of the Holy Spirit, His Word, prayer, circumstances or other people. The Lord may speak to us in dreams, visions or even by His audible voice; however, don't expect God's audible voice to be the common way He will speak! God's voice often blends into a melodic harmony to which we have to tune in.[5]

Accountability

Christians find support through *accountability*, which often occurs in a mentoring relationship. Accountability is a way for us to check up on each other so that we stay on a safe path and remain responsible for our actions.

What exactly is accountability? Personal accountability is finding out from God what He wants us to do and then asking someone to hold us accountable to follow through on those behaviors. If a spiritual daughter wants to be held accountable to her spiritual mother for a certain area in her life that needs support, it doesn't mean the mother tells her what to do. The spiritual mother does not control the actions and decisions of her daughter. Instead, she forms a partnership with her protégé that results in good choices and personal growth. The daughter makes the final decision about what she will do in any given situation. Mentors point others to Jesus; in the end, each person is responsible for his or her own decisions.

The truth of Galatians 4:2, that children need guardians and stewards, does not mean parents stand guard duty over their spiritual children. They don't peer over the son's or daughter's shoulder, waiting for them to make a wrong move. Rather, they help them become internally disciplined and motivated so that the spiritual child is not reliant on the mentor's pushing and prodding. Spiritual parenting is not a way for mentors to get their children to do what they want them to do or for the children to serve the spiritual parent's ambitions. Instead, parents must help the children to discern God's will for their lives while holding them accountable to do it.

Normally a mentoring relationship is characterized by deep friendship and trust, so if a son or daughter seems to be making an unwise decision or is participating in a destructive behavior, a parent who expresses concerns will be heard. Spiritual parents should not condemn, but instead confront their son or daughter with love and respect. In this way, he or she will be more likely to be teachable and open to input.

A good mentor is an excellent listener and is willing to give advice and provide guidance. On the other hand, he or she is also willing to sometimes stand back and let the son or daughter proceed on their own, if the mentor discerns that this approach will be better in the long run. One spiritual daughter says this about her spiritual mother: "My spiritual mom has a way of knowing when to push and challenge, when to allow me the time to savor my accomplishments or mourn my disappointments. She knows when to let me make my own decisions and when to guide me step by step through certain circumstances."

Servanthood

Servanthood must be the crux of the parenting relationship. Leading through service releases sons and daughters to be all they can be, empowering them to grow. I like the way Tom Marshall says it in *Understanding Leadership*: "A servant leader is willing to share power with others so that they are empowered, that is, they become freer, more autonomous, more capable and therefore more powerful."[6] A servant leader knows that the more authority there is to spread around, the more people there are who have authority. When the mentoring relationship centers on servanthood, it empowers people with the freedom to use their own gifts and abilities. As I have emphasized several times, good mentors release their spiritual children to go and do it themselves! I can't stress this enough. Approaching the relationship with the attitude of a servant will enable you to hand the ministry over to those you are training.

The Levites were instructed to serve in the tent of meeting from age 25 through age 50. At 50 years of age they were required to retire (see Num. 8:23-26) to serve the next generation of priests. They were called to pass on the ministry to those they were fathering. In this same way, be a Levite. Allow your spiritual sons and daughters to try new things for the first time and succeed. This is how the Ephesians 4:12 ministry of "equipping the saints for the work of ministry" is supposed to work. This kind of apprenticeship-modeling-discipleship-rolled-up-in-one is how new generations of spiritual mentors are trained!

Vulnerability

At the Last Supper, Jesus took off His outer garment and knelt down to wash the disciples' feet, saying, "For I have given you an example, that you should do as I have done to you" (John 13:15). Before an individual can serve others, she or he must take off his or her "outer garments." Although an outer garment is usually cast off when we are ready to get to some serious work, we can also look at the outer garment as a metaphor for the "Sunday-best behavior" we must cast off to enter into real family relationships. Sometimes our outer garment is a cover-up to hide our vulnerabilities. We don't want others to see our weaknesses, so we keep our outer garments pulled around us, intact and stiff, getting in the way of real relationship.

Opening up our lives to others is a complex and risky proposition. But honesty is humbling and liberating. A "performance mentality" will go out the door when we share our real, uncloaked lives with others. Uncloaked, we will no longer serve because we think it is required of us but because we love as God loved us.

Effective spiritual mentoring involves a commitment to vulnerability, a willingness to open our lives to one another and acceptance of the other person without reservation. A spiritual parent is not afraid to take the risk to share his life openly with another. Transparency leads to intimacy. If parents are free to reveal their true feelings, their children learn to open up, too. Spiritual mentors do not hesitate to talk about their failures as well as their successes. People identify with them when they see weaknesses, because everyone has them! Mentors are willing to say, "Follow me as I, a sinful human being, follow Christ."

Early in our marriage, LaVerne and I went to see a marriage counselor because we recognized that our marriage relationship was empty on the inside. We were no longer connecting emotionally, and we both wondered if we had married the wrong person. Being open about this time in our lives has encouraged many married couples to get the help they need when facing a crisis in their marriage.

Spiritual sons or daughters will not think less of their mentors when they know their struggles—they will just be relieved that they are normal! If they know their mentor is human, they won't be tempted to put their spiritual father or mother up on a pedestal. And neither will a spiritual son or daughter feel alone in their own struggles.

Jane describes the relief she felt when "the giant of a spiritual woman" she looked to as a mentor revealed that even her 30-year marriage experienced bumps in the road when she and her husband did not see eye to eye. "Just hearing her admit to her unspiritual thoughts helped me to see that she was learning to live in the grace of God in her marriage too, and I was not alone in my problems," said Jane. The younger woman was relieved and encouraged because her spiritual mother dared to say, "I am committed to Jesus Christ, and I'm going to be honest with you about how I struggle sometimes to live my Christian life."

If we want our spiritual sons and daughters to be open with us, we need to be open with them. My friend Carl was leading a small group of believers in his home, and he asked if anyone had any needs they could pray about. The room was silent. So Carl opened up his heart and began to share some personal struggles and asked them to pray for him. He told me that what happened next was amazing: Within a few minutes, everybody in the room had a problem and asked for prayer. Carl opened the door to genuine sharing by modeling openness and vulnerability.

Timing is vital to keep in mind when it comes to fostering vulnerability and expecting people to open their lives to us. We earn the right to speak into people's lives, and earning takes time. As long as the earth remains, Genesis 8:22 tells us, there will be seasons. Life is filled with seasons of time. I would never think to swim in a lake during our cold Pennsylvanian wintertime; it is simply the wrong season to do it. Likewise, in the summertime, my snow shovel is put away. I don't need it until the winter piles heaps of snow on my driveway.

God's timing is paramount. His timetable or schedule is much better than ours, and He is much more concerned about the process than the end result. God sees a beautiful diamond in each one of us, but it takes time for Him to cut out those impurities in our lives to make us sparkle and reflect Jesus. Anything the Lord can find in our lives that does not look like Jesus must go.

141

of this process, the Lord uses relationships with
are transparent and open with the believers clos-
, including your spiritual children, you are refined.
The more you are open with those you mentor, the more they
will be open with you. As you both share from your heart and
challenge one another to grow closer to Jesus, you shine and
reflect His image more and more clearly.

Asking Vital Questions

Mentoring with accountability is done with patience and love.
Ask your sons or daughters questions to spur them on to new
spiritual heights:

- How is your relationship with Jesus?
- How has He been speaking to you through His Word?
- What are some areas in your life that He is pressing
  His finger on?
- What are some areas of concern the Father has placed
  in you to be praying about?
- Has your thought life been pure?
- What sin has tempted you this week?
- What struggles are you having in your life?
- In what ways have you stepped out in faith lately?
- Have you shared your faith this week?
- Are you serving others in love?
- What was your greatest joy this week?
- What was your biggest disappointment?
- What do you see yourself doing 5 or 10 years in the
  future?
- What gifts do you possess that you feel you are not
  using right now?
- What is your most passionate pursuit?
- What is your most intense longing?

What's your greatest stressor?

• How can I help you fulfill what the Lord has called you to do?

For those who are married:

• How is your relationship with your spouse?
• Have you been on a date night lately?
• Do you take the necessary time to communicate?

You can also ask your protégés about their relationship with their children or with their parents or with their church. Questions similar to these will motivate your sons and daughters to be thoughtful about their daily interactions and help them to be more like Christ. Of course, you will not bombard your spiritual sons or daughters with all these questions at one time! And it is never wise to preach at your spiritual children by using these types of questions as leverage. They do not need you to lecture them. These personal issues will come up naturally in your conversations as the friendship develops.

If spiritual mentors focus on these major points—praying, servanthood, accountability, vulnerability, asking vital questions and teaching their protégés to hear from God—a solid, stable foundation will be laid for growing, healthy relationships.

DECISION-MAKING
MENTORING

 Key: Help your protégé make great decisions.

Whether you are a discipler-mentor, primarily a counselor or more of a mentor-coach, it is inevitable that you will be called on to guide your spiritual children in making decisions. This means, obviously, that you as a spiritual parent need to be wise in making your own decisions before you can pass on wise counsel to your protégé. How can you make decisions according to a biblical pattern and pass on this pattern to the next generation?

Let's look at the first-century Church in Acts 15 and see what they did when they faced a crisis and needed to make a decision. Here we can learn how spiritual fathers and mothers can make decisions that honor the Lord and value each member of their family.

A MODEL FOR MAKING DECISIONS

In Acts 15, we are given a model for healthy decision-making. In this particular crisis, a group of Jewish believers from the Jerusalem church came to visit the church in Antioch because they objected to Gentiles coming into the Church without submitting to the Jewish rite of circumcision. Subsequently, Paul and Barnabas were sent from Antioch along with the other apostles and elders to serve on a council in Jerusalem because of the heated debate that ensued:

> So, being sent on their way by the church, they [Paul and Barnabas] passed through Phoenicia and Samaria, describing the conversion of the Gentiles; and they caused great joy to all the brethren. And when they had come to Jerusalem, they were received by the church and the apostles and the elders; and they reported all things that God had done with them. But some of the sect of the Pharisees who believed rose up, saying, "It is necessary to circumcise them, and to command them to keep the law of Moses" (vv. 3-5, NKJV).

As the apostles and elders came together in Jerusalem, they first shared what they had experienced with the Church. Then they meet with the leadership (the apostles and elders) to consider the matter, and there was quite a bit of wrangling and argument from those on both sides of the question. Finally, Peter rose up and said to them:

> Men and brethren, you know that a good while ago God chose among us, that by my mouth the Gentiles should hear the word of the gospel and believe. So God, who knows the heart, acknowledged them by giving them the Holy Spirit, just as He did to us, and made no distinction between us and them, purifying their hearts by faith (vv. 7-9, NKJV).

Peter reminded these Jewish believers that they were saved by faith and faith alone, just as the Gentile believers were. When he was finished speaking, the multitude kept silent and listened to Barnabas and Paul testify about the many miracles and wonders God had worked through them among the Gentiles (see v. 12). After Peter, Paul and Barnabas had their say, James, the head elder and apostolic leader of the Jerusalem church, spoke up. The Early Church leaders trusted James because they were in his field of authority and responsibility.

First, James reviewed what he had heard from various leaders throughout the meeting together. Second, he quoted from the Scriptures. Finally, he spoke up in favor of accepting the uncircumcised Gentiles: "Therefore I judge that we should not trouble those from among the Gentiles who are turning to God" (v. 19, *NKJV*).

The apostles, elders and the whole congregation agreed with James's wise words and decided to send delegates to Antioch and throughout the other city-churches to report the decision with an "acceptance letter." A church doctrinal issue was resolved!

What can we learn about decision-making from this story?

PRINCIPLES FOR MAKING DECISIONS

I believe this Early Church issue was resolved because God's leaders followed proper biblical decision-making principles. As we look at this story carefully, we see three principles of godly decision-making, and I believe the combined strengths of these three principles can help us make wise decisions at any level of leadership.

1. God speaks through a leader (father or mother).
2. God speaks through the team.
3. God speaks through His people.

Trouble often comes when one of these principles is given greater precedence than the others. Practicing only one of these principles is like driving in a rut on the side of the road rather than utilizing the total road; it causes a spiritual parent to lead in a lopsided manner, often making poor decisions. These three principles are meant to complement each other, as each level of leadership works together in relationship with one another.

To help us better understand the dynamics between all three principles, let's think for a minute about the options a natural family has if they utilize one or more of these principles while planning a vacation. Let's say the Mancini family wants to make a decision about where to spend their summer vacation. Who should make the decision? Should Dad make a decision to go on a fishing vacation without taking the rest of his family into consideration? Should Mom and Dad discuss the issue thoroughly and then give up the idea entirely when they cannot agree? Should the children vote and decide by democratic majority where to go? Or is there a better way?

As we take a closer look at and apply the three decision-making principles, you decide.

1. God Speaks Through a Leader

God always calls and anoints someone to lead the way. Although God may speak His vision and direction through many, someone is always appointed by the Lord to be the primary spokesperson for the vision. He has a responsibility that is greater than the others on the team to see the vision fulfilled. James was the head elder and apostle at Jerusalem who held this role. You could say James was the *father* or *primary vision carrier* for the group. He was the one who heard what the Lord was saying through the entire team and declared what He believed the Lord was saying to the Church.

Both the Old and New Testaments give numerous examples of this "leader who leads the way" principle: Adam, Noah, Abraham, Joseph, Deborah, Gideon, David, Jesus, Peter, James,

Paul—the list goes on and on. Moses asked the Lord to appoint a man over the congregation in Numbers 27:16. In Acts 13:1-4, Barnabas and Saul were sent out with a team to evangelize and plant new churches, but by verse 13 of that chapter, the Bible says that "Paul and his companions" went to the next city. Paul had become the clear and primary leader of the team.

In the corporate world, we often call the leader of a corporation the Chief Executive Officer (CEO). CEOs are responsible for the vision and general oversight of their company: what goes on within its doors, how it will grow and what will be its overall image. They have authority to make decisions that affect the future of the company, and their position is usually equated with power and prestige.

Spiritual leaders, on the other hand, lead in a totally different manner. Though they are also in positions of authority and are responsible for the people the Lord has placed within their care, they do not lead as domineering CEOs. Leaders who lead as fathers support their spiritual children in order to see their *children* fulfill *their* dreams and visions. They encourage their children to hear from God and make their own decisions rather than always handing down decisions made at the top.

Misguided CEOs often *use* people, but spiritual fathers and mothers *serve* people. A true Christian leader's rights decrease as he takes up his position of authority, and his responsibilities increase. His rights decrease because Christian leadership involves not power or prestige but servanthood, the mark of a leader deeply committed to the development of others. Servant leadership takes its example from Christ, the master leader, when He demonstrated that He "did not come to be served, but to serve" (Mark 10:45).

In a family, fathers should be willing to serve by making final decisions: "For the husband is the head of the wife as Christ is the head of the church, his body, of which he is the

Savior" (Eph. 5:23). In every team, there is always someone the Lord places as the leader for that team. In the case of the husband and wife, the Bible says the husband is the head of the wife. He's the one who is called to love his wife the same way Jesus Christ loves His Church and gave His life for it. The husband is also the one who is responsible to lead the process of decision-making in the home. If a final decision must be made, he is responsible to make the decision in harmony with his family and in such a way that values them.

A few years ago, LaVerne and I came to a decision-making impasse regarding whether or not one of our children should be enrolled in a public school or a Christian school. We prayed and waited before the Lord for an answer, but could not clearly hear the voice of the Lord. Finally LaVerne told me, "Honey, you are the head of our home, and I believe you will hear what the Lord is saying in this situation. I will honor your decision." In the end, the decision I felt God was leading me to make was the right one.

A godly father never throws his weight around as a leader. The apostle Paul, a respected leader in the Early Church, set an example for leaders as a servant called by the Lord to be a spiritual father: "We were not looking for praise from men, not from you or anyone else. As apostles of Christ we could have been a burden to you, but we were gentle among you, like a mother caring for her little children" (1 Thess. 2:6-7). Paul's letters were written from a loving spiritual parent's perspective, and he modeled the life of a servant to those he spiritually fathered.

Having said all this, there is a danger for those who lead solely through this principle of decision-making: They become autocratic. Abuses of this kind of leadership breed Jim Jones-type cult leaders, husbands who abuse their wives, and spiritual parents who believe they have a right to tell their spiritual children what to do in a way that violates their personal authority and responsibility before the Lord. That's why the biblical process—the three principles of decision-making—is so important. When used in tandem, they bring harmony and peace to the entire family.

The Mancini family wants harmony and peace on their family vacation. They seek to honor each other in planning a vacation. If truth be told, Dad wants to go on a fishing trip. Dad knows that he can convince the rest of the family to go to the mountains, where he envisions lazy days spent by a cool stream with no distractions or work to do. But Dad also knows that going into a secluded spot in the mountains appeals only to him. It would yield grumpy and whiny children who would be bored and a wife who wouldn't get enough of his attention when he went off to find a fishing stream.

So as the leader of his family, Dad decides to give up his rights to make the decision by himself and instead serve his family by asking his wife and children for their suggestions to see what *their* dreams are for an enjoyable family vacation. Dad knows that his first priority is to talk to his wife. They are a team, and he wants to honor her and her wishes for the vacation.

2. God Speaks Through the Team

Although it is clear from Acts 15 that James was the primary leader in the Jerusalem church, it is important to see that James did not make decisions alone. The other apostles and elders met with him, and they worked together as a team to make a decision. James listened to what the Lord was saying through the entire team. The other apostles and elders were honored because they were involved in the process and their input was valued. In this way, they were all able to confirm James's final decision.

In families, the Lord has called husbands and wives to submit to each other. God wants husbands and wives to be in unity and work as a team: "Submit to one another out of reverence for Christ" (Eph. 5:21).

We see this team leadership modeled many times in both the Old and New Testaments. Leaders rarely worked alone, but most often with a team of leaders who served with them. Moses, Aaron and Miriam worked together as a team to lead the children of Israel from captivity in Egypt, as we read in Exodus. Acts 16:4 speaks of "apostles and elders," and in 1 Peter 5, the plural "elders" is used again. In Titus 1:5, Paul exhorts Titus to appoint elders in every town, and we read that Paul and Barnabas appointed elders in every church (see Acts 14:23) to work as an eldership team.

Why is it so important to work together as a team? A primary leader has only so many gifts to lead God's people. According to the Bible, no matter how spiritual we think we are, "we know in part and we prophesy in part" (1 Cor. 13:9). A team of leaders fills in the gaps for the primary leader's limitations and the limitations of other members.

The primary leader has only a portion of the Lord's wisdom. A leader and his team listen to what the Lord says through each person on the team, and then the primary leader receives the grace to discern what the Lord is saying.

When a plane is in flight, the pilot, copilot and flight attendants all work together as a team to ensure that the passengers reach their destination safely and comfortably. But during take-off, landing and times of turbulence or crisis, the other members of the team step back while the pilot takes clear leadership—and everyone on the plane is glad that he does!

A few years ago (a few months before 9/11), I was on a flight that had just left the airport when a man seated in the rear of the plane went wild. He was visibly drunk and was pushing flight attendants, pulling the phone off the wall and cursing everyone in sight. Passengers seated in the rear of the plane moved out of their seats in fear.

One of the pilots came to the back of the plane to find out what was happening, and I met him in the aisle. "Could we help you, sir?" I asked.

"Yes, you can," the pilot said. "I need some strong men to help me handcuff that man before he hurts someone." I asked a few of my friends on board to help. We grabbed the man and held his hands behind his back as he was handcuffed, and then pushed him back into his seat and secured him in his seatbelt. He struggled furiously to get out of his seat, so we held him down with rolled up blankets for the next few hours, making sure he did not rip the seat off the floor and hurt someone. It was not your average flight! We were a team—the pilots, the flight attendants and my friends on board.

After a few hours, the pilot decided to make an emergency landing in Anchorage, Alaska, where the FBI escorted the troubled man off the plane. As the plane came to a stop in the airport, the captain of the crew came to the back of the plane once more. We had spent the past few hours working as a team, but under his direction. When the captain showed up, we deferred to him. He was the primary leader, and we trusted him to make the right decisions for our safety.

By the way, they gave us a cup of coffee for helping them out. Wasn't that nice? After the plane was again in the air, the purser and flight attendants came and thanked us for helping. "Is there anything we can do for you?" they asked.

I told them, "I'd like upgrades for the rest of my life." They smiled and told me that was not possible, but they did give each of our team members an upgrade on our flight home. We all felt like big shots. My daughter Katrina now tells my friends, "Dad will do anything for an upgrade!"

Mr. Mancini believes that husbands and wives should submit to each other out of reverence for Christ. He knows that he cannot make a heavy-handed decision about their family vacation without discussing and planning it with his right-hand team member—his wife. His wife has valuable insights to bring to the table about what she and their children really would enjoy. She makes it known that she really would enjoy a vacation at the beach. Now they are looking at two very divergent landscapes—the mountains or the beach! How can they merge the two?

Dad and Mom take a few days to pray about the decision they must make. After praying, they both come to the conclusion that they could travel to a state park just on the edge of the state's coastline, where they could have the best of both worlds—fishing in a fresh-water stream in a wooded campsite and a couple of miles drive to the ocean, with some days at the beach as well. They decide to present their dual vacation ideas to their children to see what they have to say.

3. God Speaks Through His People

Wise parents listen to their children before making decisions that affect the family. Spiritual fathers take the time to hear the heart's cry of their spiritual children because they love them, believe the Lord speaks through them, and want to see them fulfill their destiny in God.

In Acts 6, we read about the choosing of leaders we sometimes call "deacons":

And the twelve summoned the congregation of the disciples and said, "It is not desirable for us to neglect the word of God in order to serve tables. But select from among you, brethren, seven men of good reputation, full of the Spirit and of wisdom, whom we may put in charge of this task. But we will devote ourselves to prayer, and to the ministry of the word." And the statement found approval with the whole congregation; and they chose Stephen, a man full of faith and of the Holy Spirit, and Philip, Prochorus, Nicanor, Timon, Parmenas and Nicolas, a proselyte from Antioch. And these they brought before the apostles; and after praying, they laid their hands on them (Acts 6:2-6, *NASB*).

Who chose the deacons? Scripture says *the people* chose seven men, and the apostles appointed them.

During the council in Jerusalem regarding circumcision for the Gentile converts, James not only heard from his fellow apostles and elders, but he also heard many stories from Paul and Barnabas about the signs and wonders God had performed among the new Gentile believers. These stories were testimony from God's people, and James took them into account when making his decision.

Wise leaders listen to what God says through His people. Receive input from those you serve before making a decision that affects them. In the church, wise leaders should publicly share the facts and receive godly input so as to leave no room for doubt and discontent among the congregation. In a natural or spiritual family, everyone's views and feelings should be taken into account. In this way, members know they are valued and cared for. Leaders must value the people they serve!

The Mancini children listen to what Dad and Mom have to say about their upcoming vacation. They know just how much Dad loves to fish and how much Mom loves the ocean. They are reassured to know that Dad and Mom have come together in unity to try to make a decision that is best for the whole family. They also have their own opinions about what they would love to do on the vacation. An amusement park or water park somewhere near their vacation destination would be cool! They want more activity and action!

Dad and Mom listen to their kids. Together, they surf the Internet. *Voilà!* There is a water park and an amusement park within several miles of their final destination. The decision is made. Dad has served his family by listening to them and their ideas. His family trusts him because he did not try to make the decision on his own but instead wanted to see his family fulfill their dream vacation together.

BALANCING THE PRINCIPLES OF DECISION-MAKING

A leader must make the effort to focus on all three decision-making principles in order to make balanced decisions. There are strengths in all three, and if a leader combines these strengths, he or she will experience tremendous unity in his or her sphere of influence.

Sometimes the analogy of *head*, *shoulders* and *body* is used to show the combined strength of all three principles. This image helps to explain further how a spiritual leader works with others to hear what the Lord is saying.

Psalm 133 is a song about unity. At that point in biblical history, Israel was united under one head: David. The blessing of this unity is imagined in the psalm as the fragrant, holy anointing oil poured upon the head of Aaron, the high priest. The oil was so plentiful that it ran down his face, onto his shoulders and over his garment. God pours out His wisdom on the head, which flows to the shoulders and onto the body.

Applying this analogy to balanced decision-making, the head (primary leader) of every team must be properly attached to the shoulders (the others on the team) and the body (the people) through God-ordained relationships of trust and affirmation. If the head is appropriately attached to the shoulders by servanthood, prayer and proper communication, and the shoulders properly support and affirm the head, there will be unity, and God will command a blessing as indicated in Psalm 133. God pours out His grace and anointing to the primary leader of the team to hear what He is saying through the entire team.

However, if the head is stretched too far from the shoulders—that is, the primary leader does not honor the team—and makes decisions in an autocratic style, the shoulders (the team) and the body (the people) experience a pain in the neck! By the same token, if the head is forced down through a lack of honor from the shoulders or the body, nobody will get very far. Unless there is trust established between team members and team leaders, decisions cannot be made effectively.

The head is committed to value the shoulders and the body for good decision-making. Wise leaders who are in the role of authority will also pursue authentic accountability relationships with spiritual fathers or mothers that the Lord has placed in their lives. This will help leaders avoid the "absolute authority" trap. (A complete discussion of how these principles apply to church leadership can be found in a book I authored with three friends, titled *The Biblical Role of Elders for Today's Church*.[1])

When brothers "dwell together in unity" (Ps. 133:1), the Lord commands a blessing.

PASSING ON THE PRINCIPLES

Once you have adopted the three biblical principles into your decision-making, let your spiritual children see you applying them to your life. Talk about the principles so that your protégé begins to identify them at work as you make decisions that affect your spiritual family.

When it comes time for your son or daughter to make a decision, help him or her apply the principles to his or her own life. Help them to seek the input of everyone impacted by the decision, to pray for the Lord's guidance and direction, and then move forward in confidence.

The key to all decision-making is knowing that only the Lord can give us wisdom for making decisions. We cannot lean on our own understanding, as the writer of Proverbs admonishes us: "Trust in the LORD with all your heart, and do not lean on your own understanding. In all your ways acknowledge Him, and He will make your paths straight" (3:5-6). We must live in the constant reality that Christ is in our midst, waiting for us to ask Him for wisdom and for direction. Jesus tells us clearly in Matthew 18:19-20: "Again I say to you, that if two of you agree on earth about anything that they may ask, it shall be done for them by My Father who is in heaven. For where two or three have gathered together in My name, I am there in their midst."

As you nurture and encourage your spiritual children to seek the Lord in all things, their decisions will reflect a growing wisdom and a deepening intimacy with Him.

No one is exempt from making decisions. Every person, whether it is in the home, church, workplace, school or community, must make decisions that affect other people. Husbands and wives are appointed by the Lord to give leadership to their families. Pastors and elders are appointed by God to give leadership to their local church. Spiritual parents are appointed to give stewardship to their spiritual sons or daughters. A student who is captain of the football team is a leader to his school's team. In some capacity, most of us are in leadership positions and must know how to make wise biblical decisions.

When we learn how to take responsibility for biblical decision-making, we begin to notice that it works in the home, in the church, in a youth group, in business and in any other place decisions need to be made. God's desire is to "command a blessing" on spiritual fathers and mothers and on spiritual families as we follow His principles of leadership and decision-making.

God wants spiritual mentors of all kinds to train their sons and daughters in biblical decision-making so that they do not become autocratic leaders or live in fear of making decisions that affect others. When sons and daughters learn to hear from their heavenly Father and honor their spiritual parents and others impacted by their decisions, they make wise and godly judgments in decision-making.

CHAPTER 12

AVOIDING PITFALLS

 Key: Trust God and be wise in your relationships.

We are all held accountable in one way or another. In civil society there are laws to obey, and if we fail to do so, we suffer the consequences. In Christian society, likewise, there are guidelines for governing relationships. There are also guidelines to follow that can help spiritual mentors and their protégés to avoid relational problems. In this chapter, we will explore some of these guidelines and how to put them in place in the mentoring relationship.

DISCUSSING EXPECTATIONS

At the outset of any successful mentoring relationship, it is wise to discuss expectations. What are both sides looking for? If you are the mentor, explain how you would like to help your spiritual son or daughter and what you expect from them. Be honest and open. Goals and objectives should be discussed for the relationship. Then ask your protégé for his or her assessment of his or her current state. Are there already certain areas of life and ministry that the son or daughter needs to grow in? Are there any major skeletons in the closet that need to be dealt with immediately?

If you are the spiritual son or daughter, talk to your mentor about your goals and the kind of assistance you feel you need. I heard about a very angry son who persistently harassed his natural father for not being there for him after the parents divorced during his growing-up years. Nothing the father did could make up for all his shortcomings in his son's eyes. The father took his son's berating for some time and then in an unguarded moment blurted out, "Did you ever stop to think you were hardly a perfect son?" Why do we as sons expect perfection of our fathers and yet excuse our imperfect and immature behavior?

Spiritual sons and daughters need to be vulnerable and initiate a conversation about their needs with their spiritual mentors, and not expect them to be mind-readers. Oftentimes we hold relationships captive by our secret, unmet expectations. I have done it with my wife and with those who have mentored me. *Why not?* I have reasoned. *They should know. They know me and are older, wiser or have more experience.*

But we must stop holding people captive, end the games and cease the manipulation. If you desire prayer or a hug, initiate it! Humble yourself and stop the mental and emotional hi-jinks. They will get you nowhere but frustrated and self-consumed.

When you enter into a mentoring relationship, you accept your mentor or protégé for who he or she is. You do not compete with them. You do not have to be better—different is okay. Do not compare yourself. When we compare, the end result will be feeling devalued by (inadequacy) or better than (pride) the one to whom we are comparing ourselves—and neither feeling will deepen the relationship. Comparison will undermine any and all accomplishments. Remember, this is a give-and-take relationship. We are not out to change anyone; that is the Holy Spirit's work.

Decide on some practical get-together times. It is a good idea to determine how you can best maintain contact with each other, whether face to face, by phone or by email. Both the mentor and spiritual son or daughter should respect each other's time and responsibilities so that they do not impose beyond what is reasonable.

How often and for how long should you meet? The answers will vary. One breakfast meeting each month may be adequate for some people to develop a healthy relationship, while new Christians or those in crisis may need more (weekly or bi-weekly). These planned, regular contacts should be interlaced with a lot of spontaneous contact, and you should meet both on the mentor's and on the son's or daughter's turf.

Both parties should also discuss early on if they foresee the relationship to be for a certain period of time or to continue in an ongoing long-term relationship (of course, this needs to be re-evaluated periodically). A spiritual parent may maintain a close relationship for a lifetime with a spiritual child, but with others he or she may be close for only a few years or even months. Whether it is for a mutually agreeable time period or an ongoing commitment, it is the health of the relationship that is vital! Keep it healthy by periodically examining the friendship to determine if continuing is God's best plan.

Eventually, if it has achieved its purpose, both the spiritual mentor and protégé should take the responsibility for the winding down of the relationship. This does not mean that ties are broken and you never speak to each other again; in a natural family, when a son marries, he is still his father's son. The father may no longer have as much input in his life, but he remains a son. In some relationships, a phone call now and then will be all it takes to maintain a father-son relationship. It is important that a son or daughter knows their father or mother is available if needed, even if regular and deep time together is in the past.

I have served in a spiritual fathering relationship with some Christian leaders for more than 20 years. Although they still look to me as a spiritual father, I now consider them to be my peers. This relational evolution should be the aim of all spiritual mentoring relationships; after all, the point is to grow up new spiritual parents and release them for God's glory!

DEALING WITH RELATIONAL PROBLEMS

Years ago, one Saturday morning, my then six-year-old daughter Leticia begged me to make her some pancakes for breakfast. Her mother and sisters were gone for the morning, and she was stuck with me as the potential cook. My cooking skills being what they are, I pleaded with her, "Please, Leticia, couldn't you just eat cereal today?" She persisted, so I obliged.

Half asleep, I read the instructions incorrectly and the end product looked unfit for human consumption. I asked her again to please eat cereal instead. She again staunchly persisted.

This time the oil in the pan caught on fire! I knew it was not going to be a good day. We later had to repaint the blackened spot the fire left on the ceiling.

"Please try again, Daddy," Leticia implored, making good use of her big blue eyes. How could I resist? I decided just to ignore the instructions. This time, without following the recipe on the side of the box, I got milk and eggs out of the refrigerator and began to mix in any ingredients I could find that I thought might work. Amazingly enough, the concoction looked edible. With a prayer of thanks, I slid the golden pancakes onto a plate, drenched them in lots of syrup (which I did not, thankfully, have to make), and placed them in front of my ever-patient daughter.

Leticia took one bite of my freshly made pancakes, looked up at me with a mixture of despair and disappointment and said, "Daddy, may I have cereal, please?"

Today, I meet people throughout the Body of Christ who have given up on the mentoring they long for because complicated and unpredictable situations have arisen in previous spiritual parenting relationships.

Sometimes spiritual fathers and mothers, and sons and daughters, too, find themselves in discordant relationships and quit. It's not that the spiritual parents did not try. Perhaps they read the scriptural directions wrongly and the relationship with their son or daughter flopped. Or maybe a spiritual son or daughter was mentored by a spiritual parent who sought to control rather than encourage. Yet giving up entirely on all spiritual parenting relationships because some do not work out is like throwing the baby out with the bath water. (Or never eating pancakes again because of one little house fire!)

I remember my son, Josh, playing with a model electric train as a kid, and time and time again the train would round one particular corner and fly off the track, lying helpless on its side, spinning its wheels. It could not possibly get back on the tracks without outside help. It was only when I picked up the train and gently set it on the tracks that it could run again.

It is a fact that people have a tendency to get off track spiritually and relationally. But if we allow Him, our Father God will pick us up when we get derailed and place us back on track. Only then can we arrive at the destination God intended for us. The Lord is a great Redeemer! He wants to heal the hurts and help believers recover what Satan has tried to steal from them.

Every relationship experiences rough patches. Friction is unavoidable in spiritual mentoring, but following a few simple guidelines can keep it to a minimum and get us back on track when we derail.

Be Realistic about Meeting Needs

Because of the powerful connection of a spiritual mentoring relationship, there is a danger that the parents take on too much responsibility for the growth of the children. If a mentor does not guard against this kind of unhealthy dependence, a son or daughter may begin to demand more than a father or mother can or should give. Before they know it, the relationship becomes self-serving.

Tony Fitzgerald from Church of the Nations has served as a spiritual father to church leaders scattered across the globe for more than 20 years. He gave me this wise advice in one of our conversations: "Fathering is not to meet every need, but to be sure every need is met."

In the story of the Good Samaritan, the compassionate Samaritan attended to the wounded man's bruises, placed him on his donkey and took him to an inn. At that point, the Samaritan's job was finished. He entrusted the wounded man to the innkeeper and then left. He did not meet every need of the wounded man, but he made sure his every need was attended to.

In the same way, spiritual mentors can meet certain needs but entrust their children to others to meet further needs. When a spiritual father directs his son to helpful resources such as books, CDs, videos and other spiritual leaders and counselors, he is helping meet a need without directly meeting it himself. Spiritual mentors must be realistic about which needs they are able and should meet, and help their children by directing them to other sources.

Maintain Proper Emotional Boundaries

A relationship goes downhill when two people lean too much on each other rather than on the Lord. If spiritual sons or daughters look to fathers or mothers to solve their problems or meet all their needs, the relationship becomes need-driven and unhealthy.

Especially in spiritual mothering relationships, with most women's need to form close friendships, the mentor and daughter may tend to absorb themselves too deeply. If either party becomes possessive and demanding, it is moving toward an unhealthy dependency and boundaries need to be drawn and maintained.

"Dependent relationships become ingrown and create a seedbed for one person to become emotionally dependent on another," according to author and friend Steve Prokopchak. In his book *Recognizing Emotional Dependency*, he defines emotional dependency as "the condition resulting when the ongoing presence and/or nurturing of another is believed necessary for personal security." Steve goes on to say, "It's true that we need others. I believe that relationship with God and with others is the most important thing in life. . . . However, our need for relationship cannot be allowed to become the center of a person's life. The emotionally dependent person feels as though he cannot exist or function without this relationship. Mistakenly, this association is an attempt to meet the need for intimacy and security."[1]

In spiritual mentoring relationships, we must maintain proper boundaries in order to maintain healthy relationships. This means we must be sure of our identity in Christ and want to please Him rather than another person. We need to be sure the person we are mentoring does not trust us more than the Holy Spirit.

Here are a few practical steps a spiritual mentor can take to draw and maintain healthy relational boundaries:

- Talk about mutual expectations of the relationship. As you build a friendship with your protégé, maintain a healthy sense of self. Otherwise, emotional dependency happens.

- Early on in the relationship, determine what you are and aren't responsible for in the protégé's life. Ultimately, you are not their caretaker; Jesus is.

- Know where to draw the line in your time spent with your protégé.

- Be trustworthy. Don't betray confidential information your protégé tells you.

- Mentoring is an act of service. Realize the relationship is in place to encourage the protégé in his or her relationship with Christ.

Get Outside Help If Needed

Mentors should be aware that sometimes they need help to solve a severe problem in a son's or daughter's life. There is no need to be alarmed by these situations; when people are progressing on a spiritual journey, there are inevitably besetting sins that need to be dealt with. Stubborn struggles may include depression, addictions to sex, alcohol or drugs, or problems dealing with anger appropriately. (Again let me suggest my friend Steve Prokopchak's excellent manual called *Counseling Basics* that helps lay leaders to counsel those they are mentoring.[2])

If a spiritual son or daughter has a severe ongoing addiction or emotional problem that the mentor is not able to deal with, they may benefit from meeting with a professional counselor. The mentor can stay involved in the son's or daughter's life and at the same time have the additional support available to help them through the difficult times. Your church may have a list of recommended Christian counselors, or you can find a list of therapists in your area from the American Association of Christian Counselors at www.aacc.net.

End Well If the Relationship Must End

Although it is usually possible to sort out problems without dissolving the mentoring relationship, sometimes there may be negative interpersonal dynamics that make it impossible to continue. If a once-beneficial relationship becomes critical and disappointment sets in, don't immediately bolt from the scene!

Address the roots of the conflict before it causes irrevocable damage. Be vulnerable and candid in your communication, and pray together. Try to resolve the conflict as painlessly as possible. It may be helpful to have a trusted third party to guide the mentoring relationship through the conflict.

If the problems cannot be resolved, remember that a mentoring relationship is not a covenant bond; it is a spiritual impartation into the life of another that allows freedom and flexibility. If the time comes for a separation, the love relationship we have with Christ and each other will help us to discern how to graciously and lovingly bow out. Allow the Lord to be your comfort so that you do not grow bitter or refuse to take the risk of another relationship.

Above all, be supportive. Mentors have the hearts of fathers and mothers. Their greatest aspiration is to provide a supportive environment to help their sons or daughters discover what God has for them and then assist them in finding their own answers. Lest we forget, mentors are never a substitute for the Holy Spirit. Supporting, rather than advising, honors the uniqueness of the protégé's own calling. Let's be spiritual parents who help our sons and daughters fully live out God's callings and visions for their lives.

MINISTERING IN YOUR FIELD

I live in the fertile agricultural area of Lancaster County, Pennsylvania. Its lush green and golden fields of corn, alfalfa, barley and wheat cover the landscape. Whenever I fly over the area, I am amazed at the patterns the fields of all shapes and sizes display, with their unique colors and easily recognizable boundaries.

Each field represents a particular crop waiting to be harvested. This diversity of crops gives our community the distinction of producing more agricultural products and yielding more food than any other non-irrigated county in our nation.

Everyone has specific fields of ministry, unique to them, that have been assigned by the Lord. These fields that dot the landscape of our lives are our spheres of influence, responsibility and anointing. The Greek word that is translated "field" in 2 Corinthians 10 is *metron*, which is defined as "a measure of activity that defines the limits of one's power and influence." These spiritual fields give us great opportunities to experience God's blessing and empowerment, as long as we work within the boundary of our field: "We, however, will not boast beyond proper limits, but will confine our boasting to the field God has assigned to us, a field that reaches even to you" (2 Cor. 10:13).

Every person has several different areas for which they have the influence and power to decide what goes on within those fields. A married person has a field of ministry with a spouse. If they have children, their field extends to their family. If an individual leads a small group, he has another sphere of influence that includes the spiritual responsibility for the small-group members. An involvement in a church is another sphere in which to experience God's blessing, while our communities are yet another. As a member of our neighborhood, we have a field of ministry on our street as we serve our neighbors and pray for them to come to Christ. Our workplace provides an additional sphere of influence. Spiritual mentors, likewise, have a field of ministry with their protégés in which they have opportunity to influence, bless and strengthen their spiritual children's lives.

When I was a farmer, I did not have the option of taking my tractor over to plow in my neighbor's field and deciding which crops he would plant. That was up to him; it was his field! I also never contemplated going into his field to plant my seed; this would have been counterproductive because I did not own that field and could never claim the harvest from it. I planted, cultivated and harvested crops that fell within my own property lines. A person who wants to have prosperous fields of ministry understands that each of his or her fields has certain limitations and boundaries, just as the alfalfa farmer knows that if he wants the best possible yield for his crop, he must keep his alfalfa from crossing over into the neighbor farmer's corn. These boundaries give protection to the field and must be carefully and prayerfully respected.

A police officer works within the boundaries of his jurisdiction. He can arrest only those criminals within the area of his legal authority. Similarly, where I live, farmers often post several "No Trespassing" signs at the edges of their fields, meant to deter hunters from tramping across their fields during hunting season. In life, there are often disastrous results when someone trespasses on another's field. You have only to look at today's divorce statistics to see the trail of devastation left when a married person steps across his or her marriage boundaries into someone else's marriage. As a parent, you have authority and responsibility for your own family's field. You cannot tell your neighbors how to raise their children because you do not have authority in their home. The stereotypical mother-in-law gets a bad rap as an interfering, meddlesome creature who disrupts her children's marriage. This kind of intruding mother-in-law moves beyond her area of authority and infringes into the marriage relationship that belongs to her children.

Let's look closer at some implications of sowing, tending and harvesting within your field of ministry.

The Boundaries of Your Field

Like the fields of our farming county, which are clearly distinguished by shape and color and by boundaries such as roads

and fences, your ministry field as a spiritual mentor has boundaries. As spiritual parents, we must have a clear understanding
of the margins of our fields. We should never presume to speak
into another's life unless he has opened his borders to us. In
other words, we cannot intrude into the life of another until
there is a relationship of trust built that opens the door for us
to speak candidly.

Of course, if a spiritual son or daughter who is under our
care clearly has sin in his or her life, we must lovingly appeal to
them according to Matthew 18:15-17:

> If your brother sins against you, go and show him his
> fault, just between the two of you. If he listens to you,
> you have won your brother over. But if he will not listen,
> take one or two others along, so that "every matter may
> be established by the testimony of two or three witness-
> es." If he refuses to listen to them, tell it to the church;
> and if he refuses to listen even to the church, treat him
> as you would a pagan or a tax collector.

Even then, however, we must be careful to allow our son or
daughter to take responsibility for their own boundaries and
personal choices. They must learn to live with the consequences
of their own decisions; spiritual mentors are in place to encourage and exhort, not dictate or control.

Just as in all relationships, mentoring should come with
some agreed-upon boundaries from the start. If time restraints
and needs are not thoroughly discussed at the outset, the son or
daughter may want too much of the mentor's time or need too
much help on issues that are outside the mentor's field. For
example, expecting things from a spiritual father or mother like
a personal loan or free babysitting for the kids every Saturday
may go well beyond what is appropriate for the boundaries of
the relationship.

Conversely, it is also possible for spiritual parents to over-step their boundaries and exhibit unhealthy control. This can happen even in prayer. For example, if a spiritual father prays that his spiritual son would approach a certain issue exactly as he does ("because such-and-such is the answer for everyone"), he is attempting to change the son rather than allowing God to speak to the son's heart. This kind of control is a breaching of the boundaries and is a type of spiritual witchcraft because it is praying with the intent to control rather than praying for God's plan. True spiritual mentors, with their maturity and experi-ence, help their sons and daughters discern what God is speak-ing to them inside the boundaries of their protégés' own fields of responsibility.

God gave the apostles Paul and Peter different fields and boundaries (see Acts 17–21). Paul's call and anointing was to reach the Gentiles, while Peter's call and anointing was to reach the Jews. These lines were so clearly drawn that Paul confronted Peter when the other apostle crossed over into his field (see Gal. 2:11-13). In Antioch Peter was temporarily helping Paul, but be-cause Peter still carried with him the old notion that Gentiles could not be accepted without circumcision, he allowed his human prejudice toward the uncircumcised Gentiles to under-mine what God was doing in that city. Paul rebuked Peter for his infringement because he knew God had given him authority to reach the Gentiles. Peter was interfering in his field.

Later in the Scriptures, we see that Peter readjusted his thinking on the circumcision matter. He is recorded as speak-ing favorably of Paul's work in Acts 15:7-11. God had to expand Peter's thinking because his field of ministry was so closely focused on the Jews. He learned not to infringe on the ministry fields of others, but to submit when he was in their fields.

We see many examples of this kind of submission through-out the New Testament. Although Paul gave clear oversight to those in his field, when he came to Jerusalem he submitted to James, the lead apostle in the city. Paul knew he had crossed the boundary into James's field (see Acts 15). His ministry existed within another field, and he clearly understood the need to come under the leader whom God had granted authority. When fields of ministry coexist in this way, with everyone respecting the boundaries of others, there is unity and respect for each other.

Authority in Your Field

Spiritual mentors have the authority to speak into their protégés' lives if they clearly understand their boundaries. The apostle Paul understood his sphere of influence and reminded the Corinthians that he only operated in the sphere in which God had appointed him. He did not go around troubling churches founded by others; he only boasted of the Corinthian church because he was responsible to the Lord for them:

> We, however, will not boast beyond measure, but within the limits of the sphere which God appointed us—a sphere which especially includes you. For we are not extending ourselves beyond our sphere (thus not reaching you), for it was to you that we came with the gospel of Christ; not boasting of things beyond measure, that is, in other men's labors, but having hope, that as your faith is increased, we shall be greatly enlarged by you in our sphere (2 Cor. 10:13-15, *NKJV*).

Paul was careful not to take the credit or responsibility for another person's field of ministry. He knew his own sphere's shape, color and boundary fences, and operated within God's authority and anointing for its oversight.

Likewise, a spiritual mentor has authority to speak into his protégé's life because he has taken responsibility for his spiritual growth. In general, the mentor has the respect and permission to speak into the son's or daughter's life when the spiritual son or daughter places himself or herself within the mentor's boundaries. When mentors earn that privilege through getting to know their children and listening to them, they gain the authority to give advice. Nevertheless, it must be done carefully and wisely.

In the mid 1970s, a phenomenon called the discipleship (or "shepherding") movement became somewhat popular. Good discipleship principles were sometimes overshadowed by unhealthy one-on-one relationships in which leaders required those under their authority to get approval before their protégés made decisions such as dating, marriage and even visiting relatives during holidays. Occasionally believers moved halfway across the country to follow their spiritual leaders to a new location, and in some cases, lives were turned upside down and families split apart. This movement led to unbiblical obedience to human leaders. Some of these leaders twisted the biblical principles of authority and accountability by stepping into others' fields and attempting to make their decisions for them.

This kind of control is unhealthy. Many of these individuals found themselves in what might be called "unholy covenants." While a holy covenant is a promise ordained and sealed by God, an unholy covenant is made with a person or group that is above and beyond the Holy Spirit's leading. Spiritual parents must not make decisions for their protégés or ask them to make unholy covenants. True spiritual parents never seek to control their children or to promote dependency in any way.

In a mentoring relationship, if the Lord calls either the parent or the son or daughter to serve elsewhere in another field, they should be released to go. We must always help others to find their place of most fruitful ministry. James 4:13,17 tells us to always remain open to God's leading in our lives: "You who say, 'Today or tomorrow we will go to this or that city' . . . instead, you ought to say, 'If it is the Lord's will, we will live and do this or that.'" We must allow our spiritual children the freedom to go, if and when God calls them elsewhere. We do not ever have authority to override God's direction, and if we seek the Lord's best for our spiritual children, we will release them.

Grace for Your Field

Along with the authority a spiritual parent is granted within the boundaries of his or her field, a portion of grace is given to do the job. *Grace* is often described as "the free unmerited favor of God on the undeserving and ill-deserving," but it also can be defined as "the desire and the power to do God's will." Grace is a divine energy that the Holy Spirit releases in our lives to help us victoriously accomplish a task within our field of ministry.

How do we know that God gives a person grace to operate within his field of ministry? The word *metron*, which we saw earlier in 2 Corinthians 10:13, has a slightly different meaning in Ephesians 4:7: "But to each one of us grace has been given as Christ apportioned it." Here the word "apportioned" is a translation of the same word *metron*. It follows that for each *metron*, or field of ministry, Christ apportions special grace.

Because we all have different-sized fields, God apportions grace in varying amounts according to our needs. Through the Spirit's leading, spiritual fathers and mothers will know how many spiritual children they can parent at a time, and they will receive grace to mentor them all well. On the other hand, if spiritual parents step out of the field of ministry to which they are assigned, they step out of God's grace—and that is not a good place to be! Good spiritual mentors remain in their field of ministry, and thus remain in the grace of God, and caution their spiritual children to do the same.

The Fruit of Your Field

When you are cultivating your field within its boundaries and receiving God's grace for your ministry, it will yield fruit. You will rejoice with the psalmist: "Lord, you have assigned me my portion and my cup; you have made my lot secure. The boundary lines have fallen for me in pleasant places; surely I have a delightful inheritance" (Ps. 16:5-6).

Rather than limit us, boundary lines allow us to be fruitful in our spheres of influence. The fields to which God assigns us are protected, secure places of growth. We flourish as we learn how to receive our inheritance (remember that our inheritance is our spiritual children!) within that field. Within the boundaries of our fields, we receive rich blessings because we are where the Lord wants us to be, and we know when we are in the right spiritual parenting relationship(s) because they yield fruit! Our children mature in their relationships with the Lord and are released to mentor the next generation of spiritual children.

I was speaking at a leadership conference a few years ago and joined the group of about 500 pastors and Christian leaders in the audience for an evening service. The moderator of the conference asked a friend of mine with whom I had spoken earlier in the conference to stand. My friend had served as a pastor in various states over the years and at that time pastored a church of about 50 people in Dallas, Texas. After he stood, the moderator asked every man who had been a spiritual son or had been influenced by this pastor to stand: Men stood up all over the auditorium! I was deeply moved. This man had learned to obey God as a spiritual parent and to release his spiritual children to start their own ministries—and the result was a very fruitful field!

Developing Your Fields

Growing as a Christian demands that we grow in our personalities, calling, unique abilities and spiritual giftedness, and spiritual parents can help their children develop the right tools and guide them in the process. Understanding these areas and tending them toward growth will help the son or daughter become all God intends him or her to be. Spiritual parents come alongside to encourage and give that little push out of the nest so that a spiritual son or daughter can learn to fly on his or her own. Of course, it is the Lord who determines and expands their fields; He is the One who opens the doors to the fields that are just right for each of us (see Ps. 75:6-7).

Spiritual parents should also seek to develop their own fields to their fullest, being faithful with the grace God has given. Timing is everything in developing our fields of ministry. Ecclesiastes 8:5-6 indicates that there is a proper time, place and method for everything. David is the classic example: He was called and anointed to be king, but there already was a reigning king. David, though his calling was clear, did not seize power or attempt to overthrow the existing authority. Instead, he allowed God to promote him at the proper time (see Ps. 78:70-72). He waited in faith and grew into the king God had anointed him to be.

If you are responsible within your present field and develop it well, God will enhance it. Allow God to promote you. Sometimes when we teach this concept, it sounds like a business principle. It is true that many successful businesses have adopted this Kingdom principle of promoting those who are faithful in the area that has been assigned to them. But this was in the Bible long before modern business owners recognized it as an effective management method. If you are called to be a spiritual father or mother to someone, or to start a small group or plant a new church, remember: Timing is up to God. In addition, help your spiritual children determine their fields and encourage them to wait for the Lord to promote them when change is on the horizon. Children may not have the maturity to see this, and wisely guiding in this area is one way parents protect their children from mistakes and disappointment.

In God's timing, He will expand our fields and the fields of our spiritual children. Our job in the meantime is to tend and harvest the fruit that is growing now.

Take Possession of Your Fields

Paul had a sense of responsibility for his spiritual children in the Corinthian church (see 2 Cor. 11:28-29). We too must be responsible and, as spiritual fathers and mothers, stand in the gap to intercede for our spiritual children. Ezekiel 22:30 gives us a picture of prayer warfare as a believer standing in the gap between God's mercy and man's need. God has given spiritual parents the authority to intercede in this way.

As spiritual parents, we must take possession of our inheritance by interceding diligently. Intercession restricts and destroys satanic strongholds and evil forces of the enemy and allows the Holy Spirit to bring godly influences into our and our spiritual children's lives. You are given responsibility and oversight for multiple fields of ministry: your home, church, business, community and spiritual children. These are your fields of assignment from the Lord. It is your responsibility to tend and develop them, whether large or small. As a spiritual father or mother, rise up in faith and possess the fields the Lord has given you!

Take possession of your fields by working faithfully in His grace and respecting others' fields around you. Christ has entrusted your fields to you. Walk in His grace and produce a diversity of crops in carefully cultivated fields. You will yield more healthy fruit than you could ever imagine!

CHAPTER 13

RELEASING YOUR SPIRITUAL CHILDREN

 Key: When the time is right, let them fly!

In his book *Disciple*, Juan Carlos Ortiz says leaders must know how to release their people so that they can grow spiritually:

> But you know what happens in the modern church? We pastors stop somewhere along the way; we know how to administrate, to help, to have some healings, or even teach—but then we stop moving. We become corks. The sheep grow and grow and start jamming up behind us, unable to grow further until we grow some more ourselves. They keep listening to our sermons, and soon they know everything we know, and then we have nothing but a pressure chamber.
>
> The pastor is not a cork intentionally; he is a victim of the structure like everyone else. It's always been done that way. If the pressure becomes great enough, the pastor gets uncomfortable enough to ask the bishop for a transfer. So the bishop takes out one cork and replaces him with another!
>
> If it is a congregational denomination that doesn't have bishops, the problem is even worse. The pressure

keeps building until the channel finally explodes and the cork flies out! He gets really banged up in the explosion, of course, sometimes so badly that he can no longer continue in the ministry.

All this is avoided, of course, if the pastor keeps on growing to apostleship and the sheep keep growing right behind him.

If a pastor is truly a father to his congregation, he cannot be changed (or exploded) every two or three years. What family changes fathers every two years? Maybe our churches are more like clubs that elect presidents for a certain term and then elect someone else. But if we are family, we are a family; we stay together. The father keeps turning over responsibility to his sons [and daughters] as they grow.[1]

Only a dysfunctional parent keeps his grown children at home when they are ready to marry and build a home of their own; a normal parent encourages his or her children to go and establish their own homes! In the same way, any spiritual leader who keeps those under his care from becoming all the Lord has called them to be is dysfunctional. He is not functioning as a proper leader. Sadly, there are many in the Church who are stunted, immature and impotent due to "leadership" of this kind.

When our son, Josh, was 15, he was responsible to mow the lawn each week—but this is not why the Lord gave him to us! Mowing our lawn then trained him with the skills and motivation to mow his own lawn in the future. In the same way, we train our spiritual children with knowledge and passion so that they will do likewise for the next generation.

If spiritual blessings are not passed on to our spiritual children, the next generation is in danger of losing everything. When God's people took possession of the Promised Land, they served the Lord as long as the leaders set good examples for them and gave them godly instructions. But when Joshua and the elders of that generation died, the children of Israel forgot the mercies of God to Israel: "When all that generation had been gathered to their fathers, another generation arose after them who did not know the Lord nor the work which He had done for Israel" (Judg. 2:10).

Apparently, Joshua and the elders had not trained others to pass on a continuing spiritual legacy. Without spiritual fathers to remind them of what the Lord had done for them when He brought them out of Canaan, the people turned away from God. They no longer remembered or cared about the nation's covenant to obey the Law of the Lord. A spiritual legacy was lost to the next generation because no one had trained them to train others, which is the essence of spiritual parenting.

After Jesus rose from the dead and just before He ascended into heaven, He encouraged the Twelve to take on the responsibility of His Church. As we saw in chapter 9, Jesus set an example for us to release our spiritual children to "go and do it." We need not be afraid of this step! We read in Luke 10 that when Jesus sent out the 72, He exclaimed when they returned, "I saw Satan fall like lightning from heaven" (v. 18). Jesus witnessed His ministry multiplied by 72 times, confounding the work of the enemy. And lest we forget, Jesus promised that we would do greater works than He (see John 14:12).

What are the greater works? We can only find out if we follow His example and release our spiritual children to multiply our ministry.

RELEASE THEM TO REPRODUCE

While in Hawaii teaching a leadership-training seminar in Honolulu, I met a young man who had been sent out of his church a year before to plant a new church in neighboring Pearl

City. This church plant had reached many young people with the gospel—70 young people had given their lives to Christ within the past few weeks! I wanted to experience this dynamic ministry for myself, so the young pastor agreed to take me to a youth meeting before he dropped me off at the airport.

We jumped into his station wagon and headed for the local school where the meeting was held. Inside, the young people were singing wholeheartedly, worshiping the Lord with their arms outstretched. They meant business with God! After a time of worship, everyone sat down and the lights flicked on. The youth pastor grabbed the microphone. "Everyone needs to be in a power huddle," he charged the group of new believers. "It's a place where you can get to know other kids, and there are people to help you out when you have a problem or a question about your life with God."

After the meeting, the pastor explained the truth they had discovered. "We have so far reached 225 young people, mostly from unsaved homes, and we've found that these kids need relationships. So we started power huddles—small groups for young people. The young people in power huddles are growing in God, while the young people who are not involved are having a hard time."

With the heart of a spiritual parent, he revealed his releasing strategy: "I've told our youth pastor that he must plant a new church with these young people when he believes the time is right. I had to tell the church about the strategy, or I might be tempted to keep him here in order to help me build this church."

This pastor had learned the value of reaching the next generation and empowering them to reproduce themselves. There is a whole new generation of pastors, small-group leaders and church planters among us who are enthusiastic and often unconventional. Though we parents may not always understand, we must always encourage them to dream big and allow God to use us to help them fulfill those dreams.

If you are a pastor or a Christian leader, let me take a moment and speak with you. We must commission this next generation to establish their own power huddles and their own new churches. We must not hold them back. Let's empower these young people and then rejoice with them when they reproduce!

The younger generation in our churches wants to experience something new and relevant to their age group. Believers in the 18 to 35 age bracket have shared with me that although they are involved in their churches and respect and honor their leaders, they believe God is calling them to something new. They are no longer satisfied with traditional church structure. They come into the Kingdom looking for reality, not religious structures. They want relationships, not outdated church programs. They have a God-given desire to build a new home.

I understand completely. I remember how I felt when I was in my 20s and the Lord called me to start a new church—a new wineskin—just as He did with many of my generation. But new wineskins eventually get old, and my generation are now the parents. God has given the younger generation the same burden to birth new wineskins, with a different vision for a different era. As spiritual parents, it is in our best interests to mentor and release them to build their own homes and reproduce.

During the past five years, I have been privileged to mentor a team of young leaders who have started a new type of church in our community: house churches, or as some call them, micro-churches. They do not normally meet on Sundays but during the week instead. They eat a meal at every meeting. They don't plan to build buildings but instead start more small churches. They are burdened to meet the needs of the poor of our community. They meet in homes weekly and all together once each month. The group that I have been most closely associated with is made up of mostly first-generation Christians.

When I was in my 20s and started a new church, it did not look at all like the church of the generation before me. So why would I expect the church of the next generation to look like mine? I have chosen to release them and help them build a new wineskin that meets the need of their generation. My role is to be a father, to support them in their dreams from God.[2]

RELEASE THEM FOR THE HARVEST

In 1996, my friend Jim Pesce started a new church, Harvest Family Community Church, in Keswick, Ontario. Jim and his wife, Deb, were committed to practicing the principles of spiritual fathering and mothering, and to date, more than 84 percent of their church membership are new believers who have come to Christ since their church was formed. Jim and Deb have now turned the church leadership over to their spiritual sons and daughters, the spiritual children they mentored when the church began. Jim's personal insights are a vivid picture of the harvest being reaped for the Lord that began with Jim and Deb sowing into the lives of just a few:

> At the start of our new church, Deb and I spent most of our time with about six newly saved couples. We not only ministered as a team but chose to spend free time together having fun. This is important. Most new Christians need more care and support than instruction.
>
> The ones we brought to Christ have our "spiritual DNA"; they share our vision and our hearts and have our full trust. Because we are like family, there is much room for acceptance, correction and patience to cover the many offenses we cause one another. They know

that we will be with them over the long haul and accept them with all their flaws and sins. We love them for who they are, not for what they can accomplish for us.

We believe in them! By spending time with others, they "catch our spirit" and multiply the ministry. Our passions become theirs as they walk with us in ministry situations.

The greatest struggle we face in fathering is choosing to say no to the many other demanding voices that would keep us from choosing to spend quality time with those special few we are fathering. Busyness is the destroyer of spiritual parenting.

Just as their name indicates, Harvest Family Community Church is a spiritual family that consists of spiritual parents and children. They have discovered that every saint is called to parent as they grow to spiritual maturity. This church is now touching the nations of the world.

Omar and Pat Beiler, who are missionaries with the Assemblies of God, served for many years in Austria. They grew an existing church in Vienna by discipling several young people from the university, and the small Bible study group expanded as the Beilers became spiritual parents to the young believers. Four years after starting the small-group ministry, they invited me to conduct a training seminar for them. I was amazed! They had 400 people attending 36 small spiritual family groups scattered throughout their city. Seventy-five young leaders attended the seminar, each of whom was already producing spiritual children of his or her own. This church, with its focus on spiritual parenting, had become the largest free church in Austria's history since the days of the Reformation—all within four years!

I believe the Lord is preparing to pour out His Spirit and bring revival to the Church in these last days. There will be a greater awakening to the things of God in our communities, and uncountable multitudes will be drawn into the kingdom of God. When the Lord pours out this new wine, we must have the new wineskins prepared or we will lose the harvest.

Down through history, there are those who duplicated the Early Church's method of meeting house to house with positive results. John Wesley, the founder of the Methodist church, set up thousands of "class meetings" during the eighteenth century, in which people met in homes to grow in God. He once made the comment, "More has happened in people's lives in close fellowship than in 10 years of public preaching."

In the twentieth century, David Yonggi Cho from Korea followed the New Testament Church's example of small groups and now pastors one of the world's largest churches. I believe our Lord's strategy to prepare for the harvest is still the same— He wants to draw common, ordinary believers who have encountered an extraordinary God together as spiritual families who will meet from house to house to disciple and train, preparing for the harvest.

Many Christians today are thirsty for a great influx of new wine: new believers pouring into His kingdom. God is placing a desire within spiritual fathers and mothers to welcome these believers into the Kingdom and train them as spiritual sons and daughters and then release them to reap a harvest. When a young man and woman come together at the altar to be married, there is an expectation that they will eventually have children. The same principle applies to spiritual families. When people are in love with Jesus and with each other, spiritual children are the result. The expectation, if we are to bring in the harvest God intends, is that these children will eventually grow up and reproduce spiritual children of their own, in healthy relationships that grow more spiritual parents.

CHAPTER 14

YOUR CALL TO SPIRITUAL PARENTHOOD

 Key: God has called you—what are you waiting for?

Being a spiritual mom or dad is not a duty; it is a privilege. Did you ever notice how many times the apostle Paul opened his letters with an expression of gratitude for those he fathered in the Lord? His epistle to Titus greeted the younger man as "my true son in our common faith" (Titus 1:4). Paul saw people as gifts from the Lord to cherish and encourage. They were not a burden, but a reason to rejoice.

Total dependence on the Lord is a prerequisite for spiritual mentoring. Psalm 127 says that "unless the Lord builds the house, its builders labor in vain" (v. 1). Unless we know we are called and unless we depend fully on the Lord to guide us as spiritual mentors, our work and effort are in vain. It is God who builds the lives of our spiritual children. We are only tools in His hands.

That same psalm goes on to say that sons are a heritage from the Lord, born in one's youth (see v. 3). I believe this means that we can start early! We don't have to wait until we have it all together to train spiritual sons and daughters. No one is ever completely prepared to be a parent; we learn along the way.

BUT I DON'T FEEL READY!

Let's look at a few obstacles that keep people from developing into spiritual fathers and mothers. Think about your own life. What are some of the things that hinder you from becoming a spiritual mentor? If you find yourself in one of these categories, don't sit passively by. Take a step of faith to learn what you need to know or to be healed from hurts in your past. Your spiritual children are waiting for your care.

Ignorance

A lack of knowledge keeps many from becoming spiritual fathers or mothers today. Many dedicated Christian believers either have never heard of spiritual mentoring or do not understand the concept. Paul told the people at Athens that God overlooks ignorance, but when the truth is made known, people need to repent and change their ways: "In the past God overlooked such ignorance, but now he commands all people everywhere to repent" (Acts 17:30). Today's Church must wake up to the need for spiritual mentoring. When we understand that God is a God of families who wants each person to be a spiritual dad or mom to another person(s), we understand spiritual mentoring; we are no longer ignorant and are responsible to respond!

I was ministering at a church in Hawaii, teaching on the truths of spiritual parenting and small-group ministry, when a young lawyer came to me after the meeting. He said enthusiastically, "I want to be a spiritual mentor. It all makes sense. I can do that! I can be a spiritual father to a small group of people who want to grow in God." I encouraged him to speak to his pastor about his desire to serve in this way. I later spoke to the lawyer's pastor and told him of the young man's enthusiasm.

With a big smile the pastor said, "I've been trying to get him to take leadership of a small group for a long time!" At last, the

young man had his spiritual eyes opened to spiritual mentoring. He had received a revelation of mentoring from the Lord
and was responsible to act on it.

Jesus asked His disciples, "Who do people say I am?"
Peter replied, "You are the Christ, the Son of the living God."
Jesus blessed Peter and told him, "Flesh and blood has not revealed this to you, but My Father who is in heaven" (see Matt.
16:13-17, *NKJV*).

In the same way that Peter received a revelation from the
Father in heaven, we each need a revelation from the Lord regarding spiritual mentoring. If our eyes are not opened by the
Father, we may be tempted to start yet another church program. That young Hawaiian lawyer saw clearly that he did not
have to start a program—he simply needed to become a "dad."
He had faith in his heart that could accomplish it, being aware
that dads learn by trial and error as they have kids of their own
and look to the wisdom of their own mentors. The young lawyer's pastor became both a spiritual father and friend to him,
and reminded the younger man that he did not have to be perfect—he would learn along the way. The new spiritual father
learned the truth about mentoring, repented of his previous
ignorance and responded to the need.

Ignorance may also come from a lack of modeling. The
absence of a spiritual mentor in our own lives may cause us to
sit on the sidelines because we have no idea how to parent.
Perhaps we never had a natural or spiritual parent to guide us,
and believe that without a father figure in our own life we can
never be a mentor to someone else.

I recently read a book for dads about training their sons to
grow up into men of God. The man who wrote the book tells
how he grew up with a dad who was drunk most of the time. He
had a father *positionally*, but emotionally his father was not
involved in his life. Yet the author refused to allow his painful

childhood to be an excuse not to be a good father to his own children. When he came to Christ and later had children of his own, he made a commitment to train a whole new generation of fathers to train their sons for God. Today, as a writer and pastor, he uses his platform to explain how the curse of a dysfunctional family can be broken when a person comes to Christ and walks in freedom. Like this example of a deprived-son-turned-generous father, we must press on by faith and overcome. We *can* demonstrate a better way to our children.

We must not allow our perceptions to be distorted or our future to be determined by poorly modeled examples. Remember, God is a perfect Father! He is the model of a Father who loves us perfectly and believes the best about us. No matter what we have done, we are accepted and loved by our heavenly Father.

Apathy

Indifference is another reason for a lack of spiritual mentors. Many Christians get so caught up in the activities of life—making a living, taking kids to soccer games, participating in civic activities—that they decide there is no time to be a spiritual father or mother. But as nice as these things may be, they can never take the place of the faith-building, deeply satisfying adventure of helping other believers grow in Christ. Choosing other activities above mentoring is often a matter of improper priorities.

When people are wrapped up in their own lives and selfish desires, they become apathetic to the things of God. Revelation 3:19 tells us clearly to "turn [repent] from your indifference and become enthusiastic about the things of God" (*TLB*).

As we repent of apathy and indifference, the Lord will give us grace and wisdom to take others with us as we go about our other activities. Jesus called His disciples first and foremost to *be with* Him. Our spiritual sons and daughters learn much more by watching us live our lives than by listening to our sermons.

It is easier than you think to accommodate others into your daily activities. If you're going to play golf, take a spiritual son along. If you're going shopping, take one of your spiritual daughters with you. I often invite my protégés with me on ministry trips. I value the time I get with various spiritual sons who join me on trips around the world.

Insecurity

Insecurity tempts a person to think, *How could God ever use me? I don't know how to be a spiritual parent. I'm afraid. I don't know the Bible well enough. I need to get my life more together.* If you feel this way, you have a lot of company.

Moses told the Lord he could not speak properly. Jeremiah told the Lord he was too young. Joshua was scared, and the Lord kept reassuring him that He would be with him just as He was with his "father" Moses. Gideon thought he was brought up in the wrong family for the Lord to use him. The list goes on and on.

Even the apostle Paul admitted to the Corinthian church that he had a deep sense of his own weakness that caused him to feel fearful and inadequate: "When I came to you, brothers, I did not come with eloquence or superior wisdom as I proclaimed to you the testimony about God . . . I came to you in weakness and fear, and with much trembling" (1 Cor. 2:1-3). Nevertheless, Paul went on to declare that although his speech was not persuasive, the Holy Spirit's power was in his words (see v. 4). He said it another way in 2 Timothy 1:7: "For God did not give us a spirit of timidity, but a spirit of power, of love and of self-discipline."

Maybe you didn't go to seminary or Bible school, but the little you know is certainly more than the spiritual baby in Christ who the Lord longs for you to mentor. Insecurities keep us paralyzed so that we never move beyond our comfort zone. However, if we trust and obey God, He will allow us to use our gifts and even increase them in His service. He will give us courage and resolution. God's love will always win over the fear of man.

Impatience

A lack of patience will cause us to quit if we don't see immediate results. Believing we will have instant success is contrary to the scriptural principle of sowing and reaping. It is long, hard work for spiritual mentors to nurture and train spiritual babies, and it may be many months or even years before they grow up to care for themselves and eventually become spiritual parents.

There are three stages to the fulfillment of any vision, including the vision to become an effective spiritual parent: (1) the honeymoon stage; (2) the trial (testing) stage, in which we feel like quitting; and (3) the fruitfulness stage.

The Bible is filled with examples of those who started out high on the excitement of the vision, refused to quit during the trial stage, and then experienced great fruitfulness. The story of Joseph is one of the best of these examples.

After having an exciting, inspiring dream in which his brothers bowed down to him, Joseph encountered trial after trial. He was sold as a slave by his brothers, lied about by his employer's wife, imprisoned while innocent and forgotten in prison—yet he eventually became second-in-command of all of Egypt! He enjoyed the stage of great fruitfulness because he refused to give up during the testing season of his life. God used this stage of trial in Joseph's life to build him into the man of integrity the Lord had called him to be, the man who could bear the fruit planned for him. Only after all of the trials could Joseph be a blessing to the brothers who had treated him so unjustly years before.

Joseph passed the test! Let's not quit during the testing stage and fail to experience the stage of fruitfulness the Lord has planned for us. Remember: The *process* makes us into the people who can accomplish the vision.

The Lord is much more concerned about what He is doing *in you* than He is concerned about you reaching your goals for your spiritual parenting relationship. Oswald Chambers once said, "If I can stay calm, faithful, and unconfused while in the middle of the turmoil of life, the goal of the purpose of God is being accomplished in me. God is not working toward a particular finish—His purpose is the process itself."[1] The Lord is calling us to complete dependence on Him as we persevere in our parenting relationships.

Fear

Fear of making mistakes can hinder us. But we can trust that our efforts will be blessed if we take the risk, even if we trip up in the process. Bible teacher Bob Mumford once said, "I do not trust anyone unless he walks with a limp." Jacob, after wrestling with the Lord and demanding His blessing, was touched in his thigh and received the Lord's blessing. But from that day on, he walked with a limp.

Peter, Jesus' disciple who became an apostle of the New Testament Church after denying Jesus and experiencing His complete acceptance and forgiveness, lost his abrasiveness and became a true father in the faith. He "walked with a limp." When God lovingly deals with us through difficult times—that we may or may not have caused—we walk with a spiritual limp for the rest of our lives. This is the stuff true spiritual mentors are made of. We will make our share of mistakes while mentoring, but we must not be deterred or become weary.

We may be doing all the right things but problems still arise. If so, we may be tempted to go back to something easier than dealing with the shortcomings of humanity. Spiritual fathering and mothering is not easy, but it *is* rewarding. Even

Jesus dealt with problems while fathering the Twelve. They all left Him in the Garden of Gethsemane. He felt alone and forsaken, but He knew the last chapter was not yet written: Fifty days later, Peter stood with the other 11 apostles to preach during Pentecost, and 3,000 people came to faith in Christ!

Hurts from the past hinder some from developing into a spiritual mentor: "I've tried to be a spiritual dad to someone and I was hurt. I don't want to be hurt again." Well, I have news for you: You will probably get hurt again! If you are a natural parent, you know that sometimes you experience pain and disappointment as you raise your kids. It comes with the territory. With spiritual kids, the territory will be awfully familiar. They will not always like what you have to say. They can be tiresome and forget appointments. They may sometimes act like they don't care.

Jesus' followers abandoned Him. They ran in terror into the night when the mob came with their torches and weapons to the Garden of Gethsemane. But Christ forgave them. God Himself was abandoned by one-third of his staff when Lucifer rebelled and was thrown out of heaven. The apostle Paul, who was a mentor to many, tells us in 2 Timothy 4:16 that his spiritual children abandoned him when he was in a real pinch. He had to appear before the emperor, and the Christians at Rome were afraid, so they deserted him: "At my first defense, no one came to my support, but everyone deserted me. May it not be held against them." Paul could have been deeply hurt from the abandonment of his followers, but he chose to not count it against them.

Our natural and spiritual children have the potential to give us the greatest joy or the greatest pain. The inconsistent or irritating behavior in our spiritual children may come from a deep struggle to overcome a stubborn sin. Don't throw in the towel just yet. Look beyond the superficial symptoms and be willing to challenge your spiritual son or daughter to face his or her problem—and then lay it at the foot of the cross. After all, it is God's problem. Trust Him to raise *His* child *His* way.

You may have some discouraging and frustrating times as a spiritual parent, but through them you will learn to lean wholly on the Lord. Trust Him to take the pain of yesterday and any pain that lies ahead and shape it for His glory.

EMBRACING YOUR CALL TO SPIRITUAL PARENTHOOD

A man of God once said, "To do anything less than what you were created to do will bore you." Many are bored in the Body of Christ because they are not fulfilling what God created them to be: spiritual parents! Spiritual fathers and mothers rarely get bored; instead, they have a sense of fulfillment and dignity. Mentors around the world are finding this out!

Ibrahim Omondi, a journalist from Nairobi, Kenya, knew his people were not living up to their potential. Having a keen interest in spiritual fathering and the cell-church concept, he sought a working model and asked to observe me as I served our new church, built on the principles of spiritual fathering and small-group ministry.

Our church had been birthed a few years earlier with three new cell groups. But we had our setbacks. Instead of multiplying, one cell died. We desperately pleaded for God's help as we reminded our people, "You are ministers, and God desires to use you!" Eventually, faith rose in their hearts, they obeyed God's calling and the Lord began to move. People gave their lives to Christ. New believers came to the cells. New leaders were trained. At last—multiplication!

Two cells became four. Four became eight. Eight became 16 and 16 became 32. The church grew rapidly. As pastor, I spent most of my time meeting with cell leaders to discuss the needs and potential of individual cell members. Each leader and I regularly prayed simple faith-filled prayers for each believer in their cell. These believers were cared for as parents care for their children.

Ibrahim sat watching and listening, and finally my African brother opened his heart. Weeping, he unburdened himself: "Western evangelists come to my nation and hold massive crusades. The TV cameras roll. When the evangelist asks my brothers to raise their hands to receive Christ, many respond. The next week, another evangelist comes to town, and many of those same brothers come to the crusade and raise their hands again. My people need a sense of dignity, where every individual believer understands he is important to God and to His purposes. Will you come and help us? We need a new model of church life."

He and his wife, Diane, opened their home for cell ministry. Neighbors and friends received the Lord, and many found a spiritual family. Cells were birthed in neighboring areas of the city, multiplying throughout Kenya and into Uganda and Rwanda. Today, Ibrahim trains leaders to start cells and new churches all over East Africa, and he and Diane serve as spiritual parents to pastors and spiritual leaders throughout Africa. They are building a prayer tower in the city of Nairobi for 24-hour, 7-day-a-week prayer, so that the Body of Christ in Kenya can pray for their nation and the nations. God is using the Omondis internationally today because they began locally as spiritual parents.

Even more rapid than the spiritual awakening in East Africa, the revival in China today is considered the largest spiritual harvest since the earliest, recorded in the book of Acts. The Cultural Revolution, with its severe persecution of Christians, fueled the revival, and an estimated 25,000 Chinese become Christians every day through the various house-church movements that have sprung up throughout the nation. There are over 100 million believers in the unregistered house churches in China.

In January 2001, I had the opportunity to minister to 80 key leaders of the underground church movements in China. It was life-changing for me. Meeting these humble men and women of God deeply moved me. I know one thing for sure: They taught me far more than I could teach them.

Ninety-five percent of these leaders, many of whom had traveled four days by train to get to the secluded leadership training seminar, had been imprisoned for their faith. One elderly leader had just been released four days before. One precious man of God who sat at our breakfast table told us humbly that he mentors the leaders of 10 million believers in the house-church network he oversees. I sat in amazement! It was as if I was in another world. I met a group of women who oversee house-church leaders, one of whom was responsible for 400,000 believers in her network. They told stories of being brutally raped in prison, yet they had stayed true to the Lord and continued to birth house churches as new people have come to Christ all over their nation.

I was asked to teach on the biblical mandate to be spiritual fathers and mothers. After the sessions, these humble men and women of God stood, prayed and repented. It was such a humbling experience. They repented because they had gotten caught up in the work of God and were no longer focused enough on the workers of God. This is a great lesson for all of us to learn: Let us never get so caught up in God's work that we lose sight of our call to be spiritual fathers and mothers to the next generation.

A few years ago, I was asked to share the vision of the New Testament Church in Auckland, New Zealand. While there, I met Robert, who listened intently as I spoke about Jesus spending most of His time with the 12 disciples, His spiritual sons. I discussed God's call on every saint to be a minister as stated in Ephesians 4:11-12. I also looked at Acts 2, which reflects the New Testament model of church, and emphasized that small-group ministry and spiritual families are for today's Church.

After 30 minutes Robert spoke, filled with emotion: "When I was 13 years old, the Lord called me to be a minister. For more than 20 years, I tried to find doors that would open for me to fulfill this call. As I understood it, the only way to be a minister was to be ordained after completing years of theological training. Sometime back, I led a man to the Lord. I discipled him and watched him grow. It was so fulfilling. I realize tonight, I no longer need to try to be a minister, I am one!" A heavy load dropped from Robert's back. The truth had set him free. Robert realized he could fulfill the Lord's call to minister by discipling a new believer. He had become a spiritual father.

Depend on the Father

I hope these testimonies about the vitality and necessity of spiritual parenting from around the world have helped to kindle a fire in your heart. It is my fervent prayer that every believer in Christ captures the revelation of the call to minister! Spiritual parents and children together will serve and encourage each other toward maturity.

Ron Myer, a faithful friend and colleague who has served with me in leadership for more than 20 years, believes there is a big difference between being a father and being an older brother—especially the kind of brother exemplified in the prodigal son story:

> In many cases, a brother will inspire you, but a father will direct you. A brother may wound you, but a father

will heal you. A brother often sees you for who you are, a father sees your potential. A brother has a tendency to judge you, while a father will lovingly correct you. A brother may condemn you for wasting your inheritance on riotous living, but a father will love you, woo you back home, and restore you.

Aren't you glad the prodigal son ran into his father before his older brother? Had he run into his older brother first, the outcome of the story could have ended much differently.[2]

The Lord is taking older brothers and sisters in our generation and raising them up to become spiritual fathers and mothers.

But it is not always easy to be a spiritual mentor. It requires sacrifice and something that is often in short supply: time. Nevertheless, when we look to the larger purposes God has for our lives, we will see many benefits of our obedience.

Jesus understood that His disciples had left their families to follow Him, and He reminded them about the benefits of their obedience in Mark 10:29-30: "Assuredly, I say to you, there is not one who has left house or brothers or sisters or father or mother or wife or children or lands, for My sake and the gospel's, who shall not receive a hundredfold now in this time—houses and brothers and sisters and mothers and children and lands, with persecutions—and in the age to come, eternal life" (NKJV).

The person who gives up his or her comfort zone will gain spiritual children! Jesus assured His disciples that they would produce spiritual children, an eternal inheritance that could be passed down as their legacy. This was their reward.

God wants to produce exceptional spiritual fathers and mothers, but it requires obedience and sacrifice on our part.

Numbers 26:63-65 tells us that out of the first generation of Israelites in the wilderness, only Joshua and Caleb were left to enter the Promised Land—they were the only ones who were obedient and followed the Lord wholeheartedly. Why didn't the rest of their generation make it to the Promised Land? Because they believed a bad report. When the spies came back to Moses and showed them the fruit of the Promised Land, they gave a discouraging report about giants in the land. They did not believe they could conquer them.

Don't believe a bad report. The enemy will try to get you to believe his lies—*How could you ever be a spiritual parent? You're too busy. You're not spiritual enough; You've made too many mistakes*—but God has called you to the Promised Land. Depend on your heavenly Father. He loves to use weak people who find their strength in Him. You may never feel entirely ready to be a spiritual parent—you just need to be willing. Ask the Lord to lead you to spiritual parents who are intent on supporting the next generation of leaders. At the same time, purpose in your heart to become a spiritual parent yourself to the next generation.

Depend on the Bridegroom

The Lord is committed to His Church. He has promised to return for the Bride (His Church) who is without spot or wrinkle (see Eph. 5:27). On the day I was married, I looked for my bride at the back of the auditorium, ready to walk the aisle to become my wife. If she had slipped in the mud a few minutes before her entry, what do you think my reaction would have been? To reject her? Certainly not! I would have done whatever it took to clean her up to prepare her for the wedding!

Our Lord, the Bridegroom, is preparing the Bride. She has been soiled and badly wrinkled during the past 2,000 years, but He is committed to cleaning her up! She will be a glorious Church when she is presented to Him, perfect in every way!

As part of the purifying process, the Lord is raising up a new generation of spiritual parents among us. They are marked by *humility* and *servanthood*. They embrace and honor their own spiritual parents who believe in them and coach them. They have no desire to build their own empires. These new leaders see their gifts as just a few of the many critical pieces needed as the family searches after the mind of Christ together. They honor and lift up other ministries, churches, leaders and believers in their regions. They are secure in their identity and in the Lord's call on their lives as they bless those around them.

Imagine with me for a moment the Church in your community in the coming days as she returns to the biblical truth of spiritual parenting. Churches in our communities recognize that there is no competition in the kingdom of God—only completion—and we individually and corporately fulfill the call of God on our lives. Every gift the Lord has given to us is to be properly put to use for the glory of God. New believers are birthed into the family of God and nurtured into spiritual parenthood day after day. True family is restored to the Body of Christ.

This is the picture that will become reality as the Bride is prepared for her reunion with Her Bridgroom! We can trust and depend on Him to mold and purify us as that time draws near.

"Go, Find a Son!"

I like the way Mark Hanby describes a spiritual father:

A spiritual father is someone whose life and ministry raised you up from the mire of immaturity into proper growth and order. A spiritual father is the one whose words pierced beyond the veneer of a blessing into the very heart and marrow of your existence, causing a massive realignment to your spirit. A spiritual father is not necessarily the one who birthed you into the kingdom. Instead, he is the one who rescues you from the doorstop of your abandonment and receives you into his house, gives you a name, and makes you his son.[3]

God wants to give us a legacy of spiritual sons and daughters, but we must find them and make them our children.

The prophet Elijah was discouraged and depressed, as we read in 1 Kings 19. He had just experienced the high of the miracle on Mount Carmel, but he fled into the desert when he was threatened by the evil Queen Jezebel. There under a juniper tree, he complained to God of his ill fortune. He was tired, weary and felt as if he was the only godly man left in the land.

What solution did God give him? "Go, find a son" (see vv. 15-16). God believed in Elijah even when he was in the midst of deep depression. Like the good Father He is, God refused to allow Elijah's spiritual legacy to die so easily. Instead, the Lord encouraged him to train a son (Elisha, see v. 19) to be his successor. Elijah obeyed, placed his coat on Elisha, and anointed him as his assistant. Once again, he had purpose and direction. His anointing would be multiplied through a son.

I find it interesting that when the Lord took Elijah away in the whirlwind, Elisha cried out, "My father, my father!" not "My prophet, my prophet!" (see 2 Kings 2:12). Elijah had truly become a father to the younger man.

As Elijah fathered his spiritual son into maturity, Elisha asked his mentor for a double portion of the spirit that was on him, and Elijah imparted it to him. Elisha experienced twice the number of miracles that this spiritual father saw. Likewise, we should expect our spiritual children to progress far beyond us spiritually.

Someday you and I will stand before the Living God. When I stand before the Lord, I do not want to stand there by myself—

I want to stand surrounded by a multitude of my spiritual children, grandchildren and their future descendants! How about you? Like Elijah, it's time to find a son or daughter!

In his book *The Spiritual Mentor*, Ron DePriest says that God is "breathing the heart of spiritual parenting on the earth today":

> A true father's heart will not rule you, but will serve you and your vision. He will labor to help you fulfill your destiny, not his own destiny. True fathers are concerned about the inheritance being transferred to the next generation. They are concerned about preparing that generation to receive all that the Father has for them.[4]

God has divine plans for our lives. I was a chicken farmer when the Lord called LaVerne and me to serve as spiritual parents. Our God is no respecter of persons. Some of us are housewives, others are high-school students, others run corporations or work in law firms, factories or department stores. The call is the same. He is calling you and me to get involved and invested in others' lives as spiritual mentors. It is the key to our spiritual inheritance.

God has called you—what are you waiting for?

THE PROGRESSION OF
IMPARTATION

In his book *You Have Not Many Fathers*, Dr. Mark Hanby explains what happens all too frequently when the Church refuses to recognize that the flow of power in the kingdom of God is through relationship:

> Without the spiritual relationship of father to son, there can never be the passing of double portions or a true basis of spiritual authority and identity . . . The flow of all power in the kingdom of God is through relationship with one another. The amputation of relationship has left the church handicapped in power. The disjointed connection in the order of God's people has made some members lame and withered in spiritual atrophy. Other members have become exhausted, overburdened with an unbalanced share of kingdom responsibility and care. To manifest a complete Christ to the whole world, spiritual connections must be restored and the balance of power shared by each member.[1]

I agree wholeheartedly! I believe the "balance of power can be shared" as spiritual impartations are passed on from fathers and mothers to sons and daughters. The easiest way to explain

how a spiritual impartation is passed on is to give you a working example from the cell-based church I pastored in Lancaster
County, Pennsylvania.

I served as the pastor of DOVE Christian Fellowship, a cell-
based church in our community in south-central Pennsylvania,
for many years. By "cell-based," I mean that everyone committed to the church is committed to other believers in a small cell
group. We have used the term "cell group" because cells in our
body grow and eventually go through the process of mitosis, in
which one cell becomes two, two become four and so on as the
process of multiplication continues. This process of cell multiplication is modeled for us in the book of Acts, where we read
about the New Testament Church meeting in homes in every
city (see Acts 20:20).

It all started in the late 1970s, when LaVerne and I found
ourselves the spiritual parents of a group of young Christians,
and we started a cell group in our home. By 1980, we had multiplied into two cell groups in two different homes. Soon there
were three cell groups and we started a new church, a Sunday
morning "celebration" with about 25 people. By the grace of
God, these cell groups continued to grow as people throughout
our community came to Christ and joined a spiritual family
(cell) and our new church. Ten years later, in 1990, there were
more than 2,300 people committed to our church in 125 cell
groups. Churches were planted in Scotland, Brazil and Kenya.
(If you want to read more about our story, you can pick up the
book I wrote about our church's adventure in cell groups, titled
House to House.[2])

Through the process of our church growing and multiplying, hundreds of spiritual fathers and mothers were released as
ministers to God's people through cell groups. Carl Good was
one of these spiritual mentors, who began his mentoring journey as a cell-group member.

Carl was in his early 50s when he and his wife, Doris, who were from the small town of Manheim, Pennsylvania, started attending our church and participating in the cell ministry. Carl worked at a feed manufacturing plant and Doris was a buying agent for a local business, and they were unassuming, quiet members of their cell group who were committed to growing strong relationships.

After a time, this commitment to relationships and their willingness to serve caught the attention of Carl and Doris's cell leaders. They were asked to consider leading a cell. With fear and trembling, they agreed to this new venture and completed our church's cell-leader training course. After a few months as assistant cell leaders, Carl and Doris assumed the leadership responsibilities for their cell. They were a do-what-you-can-with-what-you-have-where-you-are kind of couple, and while they weren't flashy, they loved people, and their living room soon filled to capacity. People were naturally drawn to them because they were authentic and caring. In time, they mentored assistant leaders in the group, raising up enough leaders to start another cell. Before long, they had launched two more cells, then three and four. Over the next few years, their cells continually grew and multiplied.

Meanwhile, our church family was rapidly expanding, and we needed to add more support pastors to our staff who could mentor the cell leaders. (At DOVE, the cell-group leaders are mentored by the church leadership—everyone has a spiritual parent!) As we prayed and looked for spiritual parents among the cells, our eyes fell on Carl, a true pastor. He was *already* fathering the cell leaders, having been trained in the seminary and boot camp of the cell group. Carl joined our paid staff and continued to be a father to the cell leaders in the greater Manheim area.

A few years later, the Lord called our church family to decentralize and plant eight autonomous new cell churches in our region, all at the same time. Who became the senior pastor of the new church in Manheim? You guessed it—Carl. Under Carl's leadership, this new Manheim cell church soon began a new cell-based church in the nation of Scotland. A Scottish couple who attended our Church Planting and Leadership School joined a cell group in the Manheim church, which Carl pastored. They returned to Scotland to plant a new cell, and it grew and multiplied, and eventually evolved into a new church. The leaders of the Scottish church looked across the ocean to Carl as a spiritual father. The church in Manheim continued to start cells all over the community, and planted two new churches in Pennsylvania.

A few years ago, Carl turned the leadership of the Manheim church over to one of the elders whom he had fathered, and began to serve as a father to church leaders. Various church leaders throughout our nation and the world already looked to Carl as their spiritual father, and he knew it was time to focus on these mentoring relationships. He served with us on the DOVE Christian Fellowship International Apostolic Council, which gives oversight to church leaders of cell-based churches and church movements scattered across five continents.

A few years ago, Carl went to be with Jesus. As I stood before his family and friends at his memorial service, I read letters and emails from all over the world from people who said the same thing over and over again: "I had been looking for a spiritual father all of my Christian life, and God answered my prayers. Carl was a spiritual father to me."

Carl worked in a feed manufacturing plant when the Lord called him to learn how to be a spiritual father. He started as a member of a cell group, was obedient to the Lord's call, and went home to be with Him years later as an international apostolic leader!

First, Carl became a grassroots spiritual father who fathered new believers in Christ through the cell groups meeting from house to house (see Rom. 16:3-11). Later, after multiplying his cell group several times, he became a pastor who focused his time fathering cell-group leaders across the city (see Titus 1:5). He had now become a kind of spiritual grandfather. Still later, Carl became an "apostolic father." He began to father the pastors of churches just as Paul, Barnabas, Titus, Timothy and many more did in the Early Church. He became a spiritual great-grandfather!

Carl did not aspire to pastor a church, much less to pastor other pastors. He just loved Jesus and wanted to be obedient. But God had plans for him—divine plans.

I should clarify that Carl's story is unique to Carl. Not everyone trained in the small group will become an apostolic father, a local pastor or even a small-group leader. Some small-group leaders will remain small-group leaders and impart their legacy within their group by training more small-group leaders, because this is their call from God. They still become spiritual fathers and grandfathers because, eventually, those whom they father in the Lord will become spiritual fathers to another generation. The lineage goes on and on. Perhaps some of these small-group leaders will develop into a pastor of a local church or an apostolic leader, but not all. We need to follow God's call on our lives and not be pushed into a role of leadership that does not fit us! David tried on Saul's armor, but it did not fit. We cannot wear someone else's "armor."

Just remember, whether in an actual leadership role or not, every believer is called to some kind of spiritual mentoring. In addition, we are all called to be mentored by those over us in the Lord who will bring loving training and protection to us.

Let's take an in-depth look at the natural progression of impartation, typified by Carl's journey from cell-group member to apostolic father.

Grassroots Mentors

The New Testament Church was a grassroots movement that met from house to house. Ordinary people led others to Christ and lovingly fathered the new believers in Paul-Timothy-type relationships by opening up their homes and generously serving each other. They shared their friendship with Jesus, extending His grace and forgiveness to the world. In these small-group settings, they built loving relationships with one another and learned from the ground up how to become fathers. I like to call the kind of spiritual fathers and mothers trained in this setting *grassroots mentors*.

When our church started, we were a fledgling cell-based movement that grew by developing grassroots mentors. In the late 1970s, the Lord spoke to me, asking if I would be willing to "be involved in the underground church." At the time, I knew little about cell groups and how the family-type relationships built there could impact our lives. But I began to picture an underground church in the form of a tree: Its trunk, branches and leaves are only half of the picture. The unnoticed half, the underground root system, nourishes the whole tree and keeps it healthy. Like the roots of a tree, the underground church is the believers gathered together in small groups to pray, evangelize and build healthy relationships with each other. These mutually accountable father-son, mother-daughter relationships are vital in order for each member to experience spiritual growth, encouragement and reproduction, and vital for the health of the whole tree, the Church.

We taught the believers in our church that each one could develop into a spiritual father or mother at the grassroots level, and we encouraged them to do so. And as more and more of the believers within the cell groups began to rise to God's call for mentors, the groups multiplied. No one was left on their own to figure out how spiritual parenting worked—the network of roots that began with a few teenagers hanging out at our house meant that everyone was connected, from the underground up!

Likewise, you will not be hung out to dry when you take the step of obedience and become a spiritual father or mother. The Lord will help you sink a network of relationships deep into the ground to nourish and strengthen you for ministry.

Local Church Mentors

Our church grew rapidly as grassroots parents reproduced themselves over and over again, and soon we needed another kind of spiritual mentor to accommodate the swell. We began to develop the next level of spiritual fathers and mothers: *pastors* and *elders*. Carl moved into this aspect of spiritual fatherhood when God entrusted him with the responsibility to oversee not only one or two spiritual families (cells) at a time, but also a whole team of spiritual fathers and mothers (cell-group leaders). Now he was a pastor-father of a congregation that was made of many cells.

This new branch of spiritual fathering and mothering released us to become eight congregations in Pennsylvania and three in other nations in 1996. (These groups were to become the base for DCFI, the international church movement that I now oversee with a team of apostolic leaders from around the world.) We viewed the leadership of these 11 congregations as "local church fathers," and they in turn regarded their churches not as places or meeting times, but as families of believers. The local church fathers were called to oversee the many spiritual families (cell groups) and cell leaders within their church.

A local church pastor has the heart of a shepherd to care for the cell leaders, who in turn care for his sheep, the congregation. When I served as a senior pastor, I often told our team of pastors, "You should not be in your office all day: You should be out spiritually parenting small-group leaders." We encouraged pastors to meet with small-group leaders on their turf. On various occasions when I served as a pastor, I had three breakfasts in one morning as I met individually with three cell leaders in a restaurant close to where they all lived. One time, I hopped on a cell leader's tractor and spent time with him as he plowed his field! Spending time parenting small-group leaders in the church raises healthy spiritual families.

Some of these local spiritual fathers became church planters and began a whole new branch of the family to meet the needs of the new generation coming into the kingdom of God.

Apostolic Mentors

When our church was 15 years old, we had grown to a point where we knew we needed another branch of spiritual mentoring to accomplish what God had called us to do. The vision the Lord had given us—"to build a relationship with Jesus, with one another, and reach the world from house to house, city to city, and nation to nation"—could not be fulfilled under our current church structure. So we gave our church away!

We had always taught about empowering and releasing individual believers to their full potential, and now we gave that freedom to each of the congregations of our cell-based megachurch in rural Pennsylvania. We were convinced that the Lord was asking us to release each congregation, giving them the option of joining the DOVE Christian Fellowship International family of churches and ministries, or connecting to another part of the Body of Christ. The eight congregations and most of the overseas church plants expressed a desire to stay together and partner with the DCFI family of churches worldwide.

Our transition as a church required us to form an apostolic council to give spiritual oversight to the leadership of all of the self-governing congregations. This team birthed a new category of spiritual mentoring in the church: *apostolic fathers*.

The spiritual fathers who serve on our Apostolic Council give spiritual oversight and protection, and serve as an outside court of appeal for the senior leaders and leadership teams of our local churches.

C. Peter Wagner, in his book *The New Apostolic Churches,* calls this apostolic movement the "New Apostolic Reformation." He says that this new work of God is "changing the shape of Protestant Christianity around the world . . . traditional Christianity starts with the present situation and focuses on the past. New apostolic Christianity starts with the present situation and focuses on the future."[3] New apostolic leaders are dedicated to releasing their congregations to do the ministry of the Church.

More than 20 apostolic fathers are mentioned in the New Testament: Paul, Barnabas, Silas, James, Timothy, and many others had responsibility before the Lord to serve the local leaders of the Early Church. Paul's letters are an example of New Testament apostolic spiritual fathering.

Like any healthy, natural father who relates to his married child, apostolic fathers influence rather than control. These seasoned apostolic mentors coach pastors of local churches, and they do so by developing supportive relationships with local church elders. These are God-ordained relationships, not built through traditional denominational structures.

Many pastors have had a hard time fathering future leaders in their churches because they themselves have never been mentored. The only models of leadership they have seen are hands-on management and control from the top. Some denominations are wisely changing their structures to provide mentoring for pastors built on God-ordained relationships, because there are many lonely leaders today—pastors and pastors' spouses of both independent and denominational churches— who are looking for apostolic spiritual fathers and mothers.

The Lord is hearing their cries and is raising up apostolic mentors who have a call and passion to serve these fatherless ministers. These local pastors need a more mature minister to sit with them regularly, to listen to them, to cry with them, to coach them and to hold them accountable to walk in integrity.

Apostolic fathers encourage leaders to press into the Lord and to trust His Word, and they have a heart to bring into completion—not compete with—the ministry the Lord is building in a local church. He or she is an equipper and encourager who comes alongside the pastor to see the pastor's vision fulfilled. As a representative of Jesus Christ, the apostolic mentor comes with a servant's heart and has a desire to see their son or daughter far exceed them in ministry.

I am especially burdened for this kind of spiritual fathering, because during the majority of the years I was senior pastor of a mega-church, I did not have anyone to father me. I paid dearly for this lack. The Lord, however, is always redemptive. He has used what I lacked then to motivate me to train apostolic fathers who will help to parent the next generation of church leaders. Today, I am privileged to oversee the leadership team that mentors the leaders of seven regional apostolic teams worldwide, serving church leaders in six continents of the world.

Psalm 68:6 tells us that the Lord is placing "the lonely in families." The Lord is restoring spiritual parenting to His Church to meet the needs of lonely new believers, lonely church members, lonely small-group leaders and lonely pastors. A few years ago, I was in Bulgaria and a pastor told me as we drove to the airport, "The loneliness I have had in my heart for years is gone. The Lord has provided spiritual fathers for me."

Each congregation, denomination, movement and "stream" within the Body of Christ is very important to the Lord. We are all needed and should strive to work together because we are the family of God! But regardless of the terminology you use for

Christian leaders in your denomination or movement, pastors and leaders throughout the Body of Christ are crying out for apostolic mentors, and God is answering their cry by raising up those willing to answer His call.

Regional Mentors

The Lord is doing an awesome thing in our day: He is restoring the unity He prayed for in John 17:21: "That they all may be one, as You, Father, are in Me, and I in You; that they also may be one in Us, that the world may believe that You sent Me" (*NKJV*). Walls that for centuries have divided denominations and church groups are coming down throughout the world at an incredible rate. Pastors in the same town who never knew one another are now finding each other, praying together regularly and supporting one another's ministries. This kind of unity is exciting!

Just this morning, while ministering at a church in the Pacific Northwest, I was asked to join an early morning prayer meeting in their city. Over 100 believers from more than 10 different churches have been gathering together to pray for revival every day from five to six o'clock in the morning. The spiritual atmosphere was sweet as these precious believers met to pray together.

Over the next years, there will be an emergence of spiritual leaders from various backgrounds and denominations who will form teams to serve various cities and regions of the world. There will be apostolic mentors who serve towns, cities and regions. They will no longer only think in terms of pastoring their own church, but will think and pray in terms of pastoring their region with fellow servant-leaders throughout the Body of Christ. Although these "fathers of the region" will be concerned about unity, it will not be their main focus. Their main focus will be on the Lord and on His mandate to sow and reap as He brings in His harvest.

When the Ford Motor Company runs a car through the assembly line in Detroit, they put it together with parts that have been gathered from companies from all over the world. These parts are assembled in Detroit to make a car. In a similar way, God has brought denominations and church families from all over the world to your town or city to assemble His Church in your region. Each church and ministry should be honored as an important part of the whole.

As we walk together in unity in our region, the Lord will command a blessing. Unity among pastors and church leaders in the same region constantly surfaces as one of the most important prerequisites for revival to come to any town or city. Apostolic mentors who serve the leaders of towns, cities and regions help set the stage for unity that brings revival.

Fivefold Mentors

My friend Calvin Greiner, a prophetic teacher from Manheim, Pennsylvania, after having served for a season as a senior pastor, now ministers in churches of many denominations as a trans-local *fivefold minister*. There are thousands of fivefold ministers in the Body of Christ today. The term "fivefold minister" refers to someone who is gifted in one or more of the five spiritual gifts listed in Ephesians 4:11-12, which says, "And He Himself gave some to be apostles, some prophets, some evangelists, and some pastors and teachers, for the equipping of the saints for the work of ministry, for the edifying of the body of Christ" (*NKJV*).

The origins of the fivefold ministry gifts are from Jesus Christ. Jesus is the:

- Apostle of apostles: "As the Father has sent Me, I also send you" (John 20:21). In the Greek, an ambassador of the gospel who is sent out is called *apostolos*.

• Prophet of prophets: "His disciples did not understand these things at first" (John 12:16). As a prophet, Jesus explained what they didn't understand.

• Evangelist of evangelists: "I am the way and the truth and the life. No one comes to the Father except through me" (John 14:6).

• Teacher of teachers: "You call Me Teacher and Lord, and you say well, for so I am" (John 13:13, *NKJV*).

• Pastor of pastors: "I am the good shepherd" (John 10:11).

As I travel and minister throughout the Body of Christ, I find fivefold ministers who have tapped into a potential of spiritual fathering that is desperately missing in the Body of Christ. They are focusing on training potential fivefold ministers how to be apostles, prophets, evangelists, teachers or pastors to others with similar gifts and anointing. They know that if they train a few young teachers or prophets who, in turn, train others, the reproduction potential is astounding.

Fivefold spiritual fathers and mothers train the next generation in their specific gifts and calling. As apostles, prophets, evangelists, pastors and teachers, they speak with the Lord's authority because they represent one of the ministry gifts of Jesus Christ. The Lord validates them by the evidence of spiritual fruit, changed lives and signs following their ministries, such as miracles. They are recognized by local church leadership and released into ministry.

Apostolic mentors train younger apostolic ministers, prophetic mentors train younger prophets in prophetic ministry, and so on, so that the Body of Christ is equipped, encouraged and comes to maturity. The Lord has sent these fivefold parents (representing specific gifts) to us so that we might be complete, lacking nothing. Their goal is to train, equip and prepare the Lord's Body to be functional in everyday life as ministers of the gospel of Christ. They mentor future leadership after their own kind and help them avoid many of the pitfalls of past generations.

For a thorough understanding of the fivefold ministry from a biblical perspective, I recommend the book *Fivefold Ministry Made Practical* by my friend and colleague Ron Myer.[4]

God planned it for us to be interconnected in relationship with one another. As spiritual mentors of all kinds pass their spiritual impartations on to their protégés, God's kingdom advances.

ENDNOTES

Chapter 1: Wanted: Spiritual Mentors

1. Erik Johnson, "How to Be an Effective Mentor," *Christianity Today*, Spring 2000, vol. XXI, no. 2, p. 36. http://www.christianitytoday.com/biblestudies/areas/biblestudies/articles/le-2000-002-5.36.html (accessed January 2007).
2. Ibid.
3. Paul D. Stanley and J. Robert Clinton, *Connecting: The Mentoring Relationships You Need to Succeed in Life* (Colorado Springs, CO: NavPress, 1992), p. 11.

Chapter 2: Making a Spiritual Investment

1. Jimmy Stewart, "Called to Worship: The Man Behind Michael," *Charisma* Magazine, April 2000, p. 54-55. http://www.strang.com.

Chapter 3: Called to Be Family

1. Robert Stearns, *Prepare the Way* (Lake Mary, FL: Creation House, 1999), pp. 101-102.
2. Dr. David Cannistraci, *The Gift of Apostle* (Ventura, CA: Regal Books, 1996), pp. 116-117.
3. Ken R. Canfield, "Safe in a Father's Love," *Charisma*, June 1991, pp. 68-71. http://www.strang.com.
4. Cannistraci, *The Gift of Apostle*, pp. 120-124.
5. Susan Hunt, *Spiritual Mothering* (Wheaton, IL: Crossway Books, 1992), p. 12.
6. Dr. Ken Druck, *The Secrets Men Keep* (New York: Ballantine Books, 1987).
7. *Matthew Henry's Commentary in One Volume* (Grand Rapids, MI: Zondervan, 1960), p. 119.
8. John M. Drescher, *Seven Things Children Need* (Scottdale, PA: Herald Press, 1976), p. 19.
9. Bobb Biehl, *Mentoring* (Nashville, TN: Broadman & Holman Publishers, 1996), p. 19.

Chapter 4: How Spiritual Children Become Parents

1. Larry Kreider, *Biblical Foundation Series* (Lititz, PA: House to House Publications, 1993).
2. Henri J. M. Nouwen, *The Return of the Prodigal Son* (New York: Doubleday, 1992), p. 22.

Chapter 5: Looking for a Spiritual Parent

1. See 1 Corinthians 4:17; 1 Timothy 1:2,18; 2 Timothy 1:2; 2 Timothy 2:1; Philippians 2:22.
2. See Titus 1:4; Philemon 10; Acts 20:4.
3. *Mother Teresa: In My Own Words*, compiled by Jose Luis Gonzalez-Balado (New York: Random House, 1996), p. 40.
4. Gunter Krallman, *Mentoring for Mission* (Hong Kong: Jensco, Ltd., 1992), p. 50.
5. Bob Biehl, *Mentoring* (Nashville, TN: Broadman and Holman Publishers, 1996), p. 92.

Chapter 7: Healing the Past

1. Floyd McClung, *The Father Heart of God* (Eugene, Oregon: Harvest House Publishers, 1985), pp. 129-131.
2. Larry Kreider, *House to House* (Lititz, PA: House to House Publications, 1998), p. 177.
3. McClung, *The Father Heart of God*, pp. 111-114.

Chapter 8: Multiple Mentors

1. Steve and Mary Prokopchak, *Called Together* (Lititz, PA: House to House Publications, 1999).
2. Bobb Biehl, *Mentoring* (Nashville, TN: Broadman and Holman Publishers, 1996), p. 179.

Chapter 9: The Jesus Model

1. Floyd McClung, *The Father Heart of God* (Eugene, Oregon: Harvest House Publishers, 1985), pp. 127-129.
2. John Drescher, *Seven Things Children Need* (Scottdale, PA: Herald Press, 1976), p. 19.

Chapter 10: A Spiritual Mentor's Job Description

1. Larry Kreider, *The Cry for Spiritual Fathers and Mothers* (Lititz, PA: House to House Publications, 2000), p. 101.
2. Larry Kreider, *Biblical Foundation Series* (Ephrata, PA: House to House Publications).
3. Sacha E. Cohen, "This Isn't Your Father's Mentoring Relationship," *AARP Magazine*, November/December 2003. http://www.aarpmagazine.org/lifestyle/Articles/a2003-09-17-mentoring.html (accessed February 2007).
4. Earl Creps, *Off-Road Disciplines* (San Francisco: Jossey-Bass, 2006), p. 51.
5. For more on hearing God's voice, read my book *Hearing God 30 Different Ways* (Lititz, PA: House to House Publications, 2005).
6. Tom Marshall, *Understanding Leadership* (Chichester, England: Sovereign World, 1991), p. 73.

Chapter 11: Decision-making Mentoring

1. Larry Kreider, Ron Myer, Steve Prokopchak and Brian Sauder, *The Biblical Role of Elders for Today's Church* (Lititz, PA: House to House Publications, 2003).

Chapter 12: Avoiding Pitfalls

1. Steve Prokopchak, *Recognizing Emotional Dependency* (Lititz, PA: House to House Publications, 2003), p. 8.
2. Steve Prokopchak, *Counseling Basics* (Lititz, PA: House to House Publications, 2004).

Chapter 13: Releasing Your Spiritual Children

1. Juan Carlos Ortiz, *Disciple* (Florida: Creation House, 1975), p. 97.
2. If you want to learn more about these new types of house-church networks springing up all over our nation, pick up my book *Starting a House Church* (Regal Books, 2007), co-authored with Floyd McClung.

Chapter 14: Your Call to Spiritual Parenthood

1. Oswald Chambers, *My Utmost for His Highest* (Grand Rapids, MI: Discovery House Publishers, 1992), July 28 reading.
2. Larry Kreider, *The Cry for Spiritual Fathers and Mothers* (Lititz, PA: House to House Publications, 2000), p. 163.
3. Dr. Mark Hanby, *You Have Not Many Fathers* (Shippensburg, PA: Destiny Image Publishers, 1996), p. 94.
4. Ron DePriest, *The Spiritual Mentor* (Shippensburg, PA: Destiny Image Publishers, 2005), p. 53.

Epilogue: The Progression of Impartation

1. Dr. Mark Hanby, *You Have Not Many Fathers* (Shippensburg, PA: Destiny Image Publishers, 1996), p. 174.
2. Larry Kreider, *House to House* (Ephrata, PA: House to House Publications, 1995).
3. C. Peter Wagner, *The New Apostolic Churches* (Ventura, CA: Regal Books, 1998), pp. 18, 20.
4. Ron Myer, *Fivefold Ministry Made Practical* (Lititz, PA: House to House Publications, 2006).

AUTHOR CONTACT

Larry Kreider is the founder and International Director of DOVE Christian Fellowship International (DCFI), an international family of churches that has successfully used the New Testament strategy of building the Church with small groups for more than 25 years. DOVE, an acronym for "Declaring Our Victory Emmanuel," started as a youth ministry in the late 1970s that targeted unchurched youth in south-central Pennsylvania. DCFI grew out of the ensuing need for a flexible New Testament-style church (new wineskin) that could assist these new believers (new wine). Today, the DCFI family consists of cell-based congregations and house churches that network throughout the United States, Central and South America, the Caribbean, Canada, Europe, Africa, Asia and the South Pacific.

CONTACT INFORMATION FOR SEMINARS AND SPEAKING ENGAGEMENTS

Larry Kreider, International Director
DOVE Christian Fellowship International
11 Toll Gate Road
Lititz, Pennsylvania 17543
Telephone: 717-627-1996
Fax: 717-627-4004

LarryK@dcfi.org
www.dcfi.org

Resources from DCFI
(www.dcfi.org)

Books

Your Personal House of Prayer:
An Extreme Makeover for Your Prayer Life
Larry Kreider, 192 pages, $12.99
ISBN: 978-1-886973-87-9
With the unique "house plan" developed in this book, each
room in your house corresponding to a part of the Lord's
Prayer, your prayer life is destined to go from duty to joy!
Includes a helpful Daily Prayer Guide to use each day.

Hearing God 30 Different Ways
Larry Kreider, 224 pages, $14.99
ISBN: 978-1-886973-76-3
The Lord speaks to us in ways we often miss, including
through the Bible, prayer, circumstances, spiritual gifts,
conviction, His character, His peace and even times of silence.
Take 30 days and discover how God's voice can become familiar
to you as you develop a loving relationship with Him.

The Biblical Role of Elders for Today's Church
Larry Kreider, Ron Myer, Steve Prokopchak and Brian Sauder,
274 pages, $12.99
ISBN: 978-1-886973-62-6
New Testament principles for equipping church leadership
teams: why leadership is needed, what their qualifications and
responsibilities are, how they should be chosen, how elders
function as spiritual fathers and mothers, how they are to
make decisions, resolve conflicts and more.

Biblical Foundation Series
Larry Kreider, 64 pages (each book), $4.99 each, 12-book set $39
ISBN: 978-1-886973-18-3
This series by Larry Kreider covers basic Christian doctrine.
Practical illustrations accompany the easy-to-understand format. Use for small-group teachings (48 in all), a mentoring
relationship or daily devotional. Series includes:

1. *Knowing Jesus Christ as Lord*
2. *The New Way of Living*
3. *New Testament Baptisms*
4. *Building for Eternity*
5. *Living in the Grace of God*
6. *Freedom from the Curse*
7. *Learning to Fellowship with God*
8. *What Is the Church?*
9. *Authority and Accountability*
10. *God's Perspective on Finances*
11. *Called to Minister*
12. *The Great Commission*

House to House
Larry Kreider, 206 pages, $8.95
ISBN: 978-1-880828-81-6
How God called a small fellowship to become a house-to-house movement. DOVE Christian Fellowship International
has grown into a family of cell-based churches and house
churches networking throughout the world. This book is also
a training handbook for small-group leaders.

Helping You Build Cell Churches Manual
Compiled by Brian Sauder and Larry Kreider,
224 pages, $19.95
ISBN: 978-1-886973-38-1
A complete biblical blueprint for cells, this manual covers
51 topics for training to build cell churches from the
ground up. Includes study and discussion questions.
Use for training cell leaders or for personal study.

TRAINING

Church Planting and Leadership
(Live or Video School)
Larry Kreider and others
Prepare now for a lifetime of ministry and service to others.
The purpose of this school is to train the leaders our world is
desperately looking for. We provide practical information as
well as Holy Spirit empowered impartation and activation.
Be transformed and prepared for a lifetime of ministry and
service to others. If you know where you are called to serve—
church, small group, business, public service, marketplace,
or simply want to grow in your leadership ability—our goal is
to help you build a biblical foundation to be led by the Holy
Spirit and pursue your God-given dreams. *For a complete list
of classes and venues, visit www.dcfi.org.*

School of Global Transformation
Seven-month residential discipleship school
Be equipped for a lifetime of service in the church, marketplace and beyond! The School of Global Transformation is a seven-month, residential, discipleship school that runs September through March. Take seven months to satisfy your hunger for more of God. Experience His love in a deeper way than you ever dreamed possible. He has a distinctive plan and purpose for your life. We are committed to helping students discover destiny in Him and prepare them to transform the world around them.
For details, visit www.dcfi.org.

SEMINARS

One-day Seminars with Larry Kreider and other DOVE Christian Fellowship International authors and leaders. Topics include:

How to Fulfill Your Calling as a Spiritual Father/Mother
How to Build Healthy Leadership Teams
How to Hear God 30 Different Ways
Your Personal House of Prayer
Called Together Couple Mentoring
How to Build Small Groups (Basics)
How to Grow Small Groups (Advanced)
Counseling Basics
Effective Fivefold Ministry Made Practical
Starting House Churches
Planting Churches Made Practical
How to Live in Kingdom Prosperity

**For more information about DCFI seminars,
call 800-848-5892
or email seminars@dcfi.org.**